It's Not Personal

*Lessons I've Learned
from
Dealing with
Difficult Behavior*

It's Not Personal

*Lessons I've Learned
from
Dealing with
Difficult Behavior*

by
Cindy Hampel

Orange Sun Press
Royal Oak, Michigan

Copyright © 2011 by Cindy Hampel
All rights reserved

Printed and bound in the United States of America
First Edition

ISBN 978-0-9845443-0-1
LCCN 2010928048

PLEASE NOTE: The advice and opinions in this book are those of a layperson and are not intended to substitute for the guidance or services of a qualified physician or mental health professional. The author, publisher and publisher's agents assume no responsibility for the actions or behavior of anyone who may use the information in this book.

Under fair use, reviewers and students may quote brief passages of this book if used in published reviews or scholarly works with proper attribution. Others who wish to use, transmit or store any portion of this work in any form or medium should first contact the publisher at http://orangesunpress.wordpress.com or write to:

Orange Sun Press
P.O. Box 613
Royal Oak, MI 48068

To **Diane** and **Walt**: for understanding...

To **Karen**: for blessing me
with your friendship...

To **Gerri King**: for encouraging me
to pursue a writing career...

To **Red, Jean, and Julie**:
for lending a hand...

To **Tina, Ron, Sue V.** and **Sue F.**:
for lending an ear...

To **Laura P.** and **Bruce**:
for embracing this project with enthusiasm...

To **Diane S.** and **Dave L.**:
for allowing me to share your stories...

To **Luke, Johnny** and **Noah**:
for challenging and inspiring me...

Most of all, to **Ray**:
for loving and supporting me
on our journey together...

Thank you!

CREDITS

Editorial assistance: **Maureen McGerty**, a colleague from Detroit Working Writers, a Detroit 300 Heritage Organization.

Author photo: **Greg and Cathy Good** of Pixel Oasis, LLC, Royal Oak, Michigan.

Book cover concept: **Cindy Hampel**

Digital graphic design: **Johnny Litwinowicz** of Grayfire Designs, Royal Oak, Michigan.

Contents

Preface: *A Spiritual Journey*

Ch 1:	*Windows*	1
Ch 2:	*Irony*	5
Ch 3:	*Responsibility and Authority*	9
Ch 4:	*Yielding*	13
Ch 5:	*When to Act*	17
Ch 6:	*When to Say 'No'*	19
Ch 7:	*Problems with Accommodation*	23
Ch 8:	*Your Achilles' Heel*	31
Ch 9:	*Not-Enough Syndrome*	35
Ch 10:	*Staying Poised*	41
Ch 11:	*I-Messages*	47
Ch 12:	*You-Questions*	51
Ch 13:	*Shrug Responses*	57
Ch 14:	*Labels of 'Right' and 'Wrong'*	63
Ch 15:	*Balancing Head and Heart*	67
Ch 16:	*Taking Care of Yourself*	71
Ch 17:	*Forgiveness*	75
Ch 18:	*Love*	79
Ch 19:	*The Driver's Seat*	83
Ch 20:	*Happiness*	89

Postscript: *A Fuller Picture*

Suggested Reading

Preface

A Spiritual Journey

This book is about dealing with difficult behavior: the unreasonable words and actions of others.

I know I'm among many who are interested in this subject. In a recent Internet search, I found 14,400,000 sites on the topic of dealing with difficult people! Despite those numbers, I hope that this book will offer you something unique on this popular subject.

This book is an opinion piece...a treatise based on the question: *When people treat you unreasonably, how will you respond?*

I've based this book on personal experience. Each chapter starts with a story and ends with a lesson I drew from that experience.

Those lessons led me to conclude that encountering difficult behavior doesn't make me a victim – I become a victim *only if I respond* like a victim. And I respond like a victim if I take difficult behavior personally. *That's why it's so important not to take difficult behavior personally.*

Realizing that I'm defined by *my* response – not the difficult behavior I encounter – became a liberating spiritual journey for me. So in this book I'd like to share some vignettes from that journey.

When I started on this path, I never planned to write a book like this. Although I'm a writer, I had intended to keep private my personal reflections and stories about dealing with difficult behavior.

I started writing in fifth grade. Back then, my mother used to drink Salada Tea. Each tea bag had a string and a little red tag that included a wise or witty saying.

I loved reading those little "tag lines" and started collecting them. They inspired me to start looking at life with a philosophical eye. I started writing my own tag lines. Then I began writing my own reflections and stories from my life. Over the years, I compiled these writings in personal journals.

Twenty years after discovering Salada tag lines, I discovered *Codependent No More*, a book by Melody Beattie. The book was cited in an article about codependency, which, at the time, was a new term for those who enable others to act irresponsibly. I pored over Beatty's book, taking notes and experimenting with her ideas in my daily life.

That gave me more personal stories and reflections to add to my journals. Eventually, I had compiled enough personal stories and reflections to write a book of my own.

I debated with myself whether to share such personal stories. Then I remembered that reading others' stories had helped me understand what I was experiencing. So I thought I'd contribute to the discussion and share my stories—along with their tag lines.

In writing this book, I've sometimes cited ideas from Beattie's book as well as ideas from other authors: Susan Forward, Don Dinkmeyer, Sr., Henry Drummond, Louis Evely and Therese Martin of Lisieux. Whenever I've drawn ideas from these authors, I note that in the text. I also list their books in the Suggested Reading section.

However, as you read this book, you'll see that dealing with difficult behavior is a subject I've wrestled with for many years. As a result, I've developed thoughts on this subject independent of other authors. So the unattributed ideas in this book are mine—even if readers may find that they occasionally echo the thoughts of others.

I think such echoing is unavoidable. The longer I live, the more I appreciate the proverb from Ecclesiastes: "Nothing is new under the sun."

Authors have been writing about difficult people in fiction and non-fiction since recorded time. I believe that, to avoid echoing a thought from the past, one would need to avoid writing on the topic entirely.

Yet I also believe it's the duty of writers to address perennial topics anew for each generation. Writers must retell these timeless truths in current language and stories. So I've added my thoughts to this subject, with the hope that my retelling may help others on their journey today.

Much of this book talks about difficult experiences with my deceased mother. Perhaps some readers may feel that sharing such stories is unfair, since my mother can no longer speak up for herself.

For a while, I felt the same way. The result was that earlier drafts of this book were filled with generalities that lacked the needed depth and context that specific stories provide.

I also hesitated to include those stories because I had fonder memories of my mother from my younger years. In fact, as Mom grew older and her behavior grew more difficult, I found myself clinging tightly to those earlier memories. In my darker hours, those positive memories helped me maintain my relationship with her.

My relationship with my mother perplexed me for many years. In some ways, it still does. Yet it also served as a catalyst for this book. And so, at the risk of seeming unfair, I'm including these stories with the hope that readers with similar experiences may realize they're not alone. I've found that what seems most personal is often the most general.

I don't have a degree in theology or philosophy. As an undergrad, I only minored in psychology. So I've written this book as a layperson. This book does *not* cover physical or sexual abuse or other criminal behavior. And it cannot substitute for the guidance of a caring and competent professional therapist.

However, I take courage from other men and women throughout the ages who lacked official credentials but wrote nonetheless—including Therese Martin of Lisieux, a Carmelite nun of the late 19th Century.

In learning to deal with difficult behavior, I found journaling to be quite helpful. I recommend it for several reasons.

First, I found the writing process itself to be cathartic. By turning a situation from my life into a story, I balanced my emotions with thought, which allowed me to see my situation more objectively.

Second, I found that, over time, journaling allowed me to notice patterns. By writing about incidents in detail, I discovered patterns of behavior from the same individual at different times *and* patterns among different people.

Third, I found that journaling allowed me a safe way to try a do-over. I'd ask myself, "If I could replay the situation, what would I say or do differently?"

Starting fresh with a blank paper or computer screen, I could easily try out a different response. Soon I discovered an interesting phenomenon: After thinking of a more fitting response, I'd usually find no opportunity to use it.

I believe that finding the new response meant that I had finally absorbed the spiritual lesson I needed to learn. So this book is a record of spiritual lessons I've learned from dealing with difficult behavior. And I expect I'll learn more in the coming years.

I've written this book realizing that we're *all* capable of difficult behavior—*especially* those of us who've had to deal with it on a regular basis. We *all* have our moments. I find it humbling to think that the differences among us may be merely a matter of degree.

I hope to keep my own difficult moments to a minimum, striving each day to live *not* from fear or guilt but to *live from love*. I admit that I'm more successful on some days than on others. But that's my goal. Thank you for letting me share some of my journey with you through this book.

This book is thin—small enough to keep in a purse or brief case. I hope that its size might make it convenient for you to read wherever you might find it useful. I also hope that, in these pages, you will find comfort and strength...*and* helpful ideas for dealing with difficult people.

Cindy Hampel
Royal Oak, Michigan

Chapter 1

Windows

When I was a little girl, my favorite toy was an Etch-A-Sketch. After learning how to control the knobs, I'd spend hours drawing pictures, then shaking the tablet and starting again.

One time, I decided to see what would happen if I made a solid box on the gray screen. I kept drawing one short line next to the other until the box was about two inches square.

At first, I didn't understand what I saw. Of course I saw a square much darker than the rest of the gray screen. But then I realized *I was seeing something more.*

By making a solid box, I had scraped away enough gray dust from one area to create a little window that let me look *inside* the toy. The inside was black—which is why my solid box *looked* black. I could also see a small gray cone, which came to a point with the tip facing me.

Then I saw two tiny rods...one horizontal and one vertical. I realized that the two rods met where the cone was...and when I turned the knobs, I made that cone move along those rods. As the cone moved, the tip would scrape away a thin line of gray dust.

I was fascinated to learn how the Etch-A-Sketch worked. It showed me that it was possible to create pictures through a negative process—by *subtracting* something from the gray background.

That was different from the rest of my eight-year-old world... where creating pictures meant starting with a blank paper and *adding* something—like glue and glitter, or marks from pencils, crayons or paint.

But it took me years to realize that I could use what I had learned from the Etch-A-Sketch to help me deal with difficult behavior.

People who act difficult communicate through negative energy. When they aim their negative energy *at* us, we may think it's *about* us. But nothing could be further from the truth.

Like the cone tip of the Etch-A-Sketch, each stroke of negative energy that difficult people add to a situation lets others see more of what's inside *them*. So when people use negative energy to draw a picture of you, they're actually creating a window into themselves.

If you're not there to provide them with an excuse to use their negative energy, they'll use it on someone else. So don't take their negative energy personally.

That lesson took me a *long* time to learn—especially in dealing with my mother's behavior.

The older Mom grew, the more she'd complain. Once she didn't like that I gave her one of her favorite cakes. Why? The cake was too rich. Another time, I gave her some homemade fudge and she cried, "Oh, no!"

Sometimes, when I'd call her, she wouldn't say that she was glad I had called...instead, she'd say she was sad because "Nobody called me today." When I'd leave after visiting with her for five hours, she'd remark, "Leaving so soon? Why don't you visit again when you can stay longer?"

I know I shouldn't have, but I took those remarks personally—*until* I heard what she had said to my cousin Dave. He told me that, when he'd visit my Mom, he'd usually bring her a warm cabbage roll and pierogis from a grocery store deli. But on Dave's last visit, he'd picked up only the cabbage roll. When he gave her the container, she replied: "What's the matter? Where are the pierogis?"

Here's the point: *When people use negative energy and treat you unreasonably, don't take it personally.* Although their behavior may seem personal, it truly is not. It says more about their internal state than it does about you. When they aim their negative energy at you, it just creates a window that lets you glimpse what's inside them.

When people treat you reasonably, they're sending you positive energy. But when people treat you unreasonably, their negative energy reveals to you a little of what's inside themselves.

So don't take their negative energy personally. We're not responsible for what comes *at* us—only for what comes *from* us. We're responsible *only* for our own behavior—not the behavior of other people.

Even if other people feel provoked, they are still obliged to treat us reasonably—just as we are obliged to treat others reasonably, even if we feel provoked.

The standard of reasonable behavior applies to *all* capable people. So whenever capable people treat us unreasonably, we can remind ourselves: "It's an emotional window." In other words, their unreasonable behavior toward us shows that they feel some fear or guilt inside.

Just because people throw negative energy at you doesn't mean you deserve it. Some people would treat you unreasonably even if you said or did everything "perfectly." But perfect or not, you deserve reasonable treatment—just like everybody else.

Reasonable treatment might still challenge you to reconsider your words or actions. *But it doesn't try to make you feel guilty or afraid in the process.* That's the difference between challenging behavior and difficult behavior.

Difficult behavior isn't about you—it's about the emotional reaction of others—and you're simply their excuse for emoting. So don't take their negative energy personally. *Don't get upset.*

How can you stay calm despite the difficult behavior you encounter from others? It helps to remind yourself that their negative energy is a window into themselves—*not* a mirror on you.

***Difficult behavior**
is a window, not a mirror...
so don't take it personally.*

Chapter 2

Irony

Once I was involved in a citizens' group whose goal was to improve the public school buildings in our community. The group hoped to convince voters to pass a bond for building improvements.

But another group opposed the school bond. I was appalled at their anti-bond leaflet. It included both a picture and text arguing against the bond.

The picture featured an elderly woman using a walker... pitifully invoking the idea that a vote for the school bond was a vote against the elderly woman. Under the picture were paragraphs that included wildly inaccurate figures about the cost for installing air conditioning in the school buildings.

The leader of that group also argued that schools today didn't need air conditioning because earlier generations of Americans didn't have air conditioning when they were in school.

That time around, the bond request failed—and the issue of school air conditioning was a big factor. I was puzzled, yet intrigued, by the group's unreasonable focus on air conditioning.

One day, I walked past the house of one of the people who had railed against air conditioning in the schools. I discovered that she actually liked air conditioning—*for herself*. Outside on her lawn sat a telltale condenser for central air—a system that had to have been retrofitted for an older home such as hers.

So I sent a letter to our local paper. I wrote that the person who thought it was okay for kids to do without air conditioning in their hot classrooms had central air conditioning for her *own* home.

When the citizens' group tried again to pass the bond, it found that the anti-bond group had lost some steam. The school bond passed, thanks to the efforts of many who worked long hours.

The point is this: Expect to find irony in unreasonable behavior. Those who protest too much about others unwittingly broadcast where irony lies in their own lives.

Irony abounds in everyday life. We see it in the person who condemns cooler classrooms from an air-conditioned home, the family-values politician who cheats on his wife, and the citizen who accepts Medicare coverage and Social Security benefits yet protests government help for others.

When people use unreasonable behavior, they may appear strong and powerful...or smooth and flattering...or weak and miserable...or righteous and well-intentioned.

No matter how they appear, notice if they:

- Do the same thing for which they accuse others.
- Lie.
- Evoke pity on purpose.
- Let other people suffer the fallout from their choices.

When you find irony, you may need to call it out—*especially* when someone's difficult behavior might jeopardize the health or safety of others.

Whether or not you call out irony, you can use it as a sign. Like those old-fashioned placards that show an index finger pointing in a certain direction, irony points you to the source of the difficult behavior—the people who are acting unreasonably.

In other words, it's not about you—it's about them.

***Expect to find irony
in unreasonable behavior.***

Chapter 3

Responsibility and Authority

Even as a teenager, I liked rearranging furniture and organizing things. One day, my mother, who knew this, told me she could use some help organizing the kitchen.

Back then, I didn't know better, so I volunteered to help. I spent three hours taking stuff out of the cabinets, cleaning the shelves, and matching the scattered glasses and dishes so they'd sit together on the shelves.

I even labeled the shelves so that things would stay organized in their new locations. The room looked good, inside and out.

But soon the kitchen was again in disarray. Glasses and dishes were left anywhere, regardless of the shelf labels.

It's one thing if you get paid to clean and organize—and quite another if you *volunteer* your time. So I asked Mom what happened. She replied: "Well, I can put things where I want. After all, it *is* my kitchen."

So it was. And at that moment, I learned a valuable lesson about the difference between responsibility and authority. I had taken on the responsibility of organizing that kitchen without having the authority to *keep* it organized.

The match between authority and responsibility is key to understanding how people create games of guilt and fear.

Ideally, authority should match responsibility. In other words, if you have more responsibility, then you should have more authority. If you have less responsibility, then you should have less authority.

When you try to upset the match between authority and responsibility, you get a game:

- In a fear game, the goal is to shrink your authority while you keep the same level of responsibility.

- In a guilt game, the goal is to bloat your responsibility while you keep the same level of authority.

The result is the same, whether you react to fear and allow your authority to shrink...or whether you react to guilt and allow your responsibility to bloat.

Either way, you wind up with more responsibility and less authority. Meanwhile, difficult people gain more authority with less responsibility—at *your* expense.

For example, shirkers avoid some or all of the responsibilities that match their authority—but they don't offer extra authority *or* pay to those who help them.

On the other hand, meddlers try to expand their authority beyond their own responsibilities—yet they don't help others by bearing the matching responsibility.

So don't voluntarily accept a situation where your responsibility is more than your authority.

Sometimes, you might temporarily find yourself in such a situation because of forces outside your control. If that happens, then you could consciously choose to make the best of a bad situation.

Then work to get out of that situation *as soon as possible.*

**Beware of situations
where responsibility
doesn't match authority.**

Chapter 4

Yielding

One of the unofficial lessons that kids learn at school is how to deal with bullies, who can be quite resourceful finding ways to practice their craft.

One of my kids told me about a bully who would harass kids before the school doors opened in the morning. Some of the kids would stand on the patio near the doors—often near the low brick walls on either side of the patio.

But the bully would take advantage of the situation by rushing toward one of the kids near the wall. Not only would that kid get hurt, but the injured child also would suffer the indignity of serving as a human cushion for the bully.

So I told my son that if a bully should try that with him, he should just wait until the bully was near—then quickly step aside.

My son wouldn't get in trouble because he would *not* touch the other child. In fact, he'd do just the opposite and avoid contact. He'd simply get out of the way and let the bully experience the consequence of his own behavior—without a human cushion.

My term for people who want to invade your space is "Space Bullies." For people who *needlessly* want to take up your time, I call them "Time Bullies."

Of course, the bully in the story above was a Space Bully. My theory is that, if bullies are difficult people who project onto others, then Space Bullies are especially defensive about *their own* space—and believe that others feel the same way.

So Space Bullies act on the belief that others will react to a threat by defending their space just as they would.

But what if you respond to a Space Bully by temporarily *yielding* your space? As the story showed, you can sometimes protect yourself by stepping aside—and choosing *not* to defend your space.

The same strategy can work with a Time Bully. My theory is that, if bullies are difficult people who project onto others, then Time Bullies are especially defensive about *their own* time—and believe that others feel the same way.

So Time Bullies act on the belief that others will react to a threat by defending their time just as they would. But what happens if you temporarily *yield* your time to a Time Bully? That's the subject of the next story.

I believe that most people have encountered others whom I would call traffic hogs. You can meet them on the road and on walkways.

Traffic hogs are people who encroach on *your* side of traffic because there's something affecting *their own* side of the road that might slow them down.

Once when I was walking on a busy downtown sidewalk, someone who was walking in the opposite direction began heading directly toward me. Why? Because a slower person had been walking in front of her on *her* side of traffic.

Instead of slowing herself down for a moment or two, or waiting to pass until nobody was walking in the opposite direction, this walker apparently didn't want to waste any of her time.

Perhaps she thought I'd feel the same way about *my* time—expecting that I'd keep up my own speed and move out of her way in order to compensate for her shift. That might have worked—*except* that the only way I could move would have forced me to brush against a car parked at the curb.

I didn't want to do that, so instead of clearing the way for her, I just stopped in place. I became an island and let her walk around me.

To respond to the Time Bully, I yielded a few moments of my time by slowing and then stopping in place. I allowed enough time for the traffic behind me to adjust. And I protected myself from an undesirable result by choosing *not* to defend my time.

Of course, people *might* need to move out of the way for a valid reason, like an emergency, someone with a disability, construction or some unavoidable obstacle.

I'm talking here about people who don't care how their behavior affects others. When you're dealing with people like that, you can sometimes protect yourself by yielding a little of your time or space.

Yielding strategically
may help protect you.

Chapter 5

When to Act

I began writing as a freelancer after Ray and I started having children. Although I did most of my work from home, I'd sometimes go out of the house on assignments, leaving a sitter with my then-little boys, Luke and John.

On one occasion, I was working as a subcontractor with another writer on a bid for a contract with a medium-sized business.

We arrived at the corporate office, stood around and chatted with some employees while we waited for one of the corporate officers to join the meeting. He was to be "the decider."

Finally, he walked in. Realizing I was one of the potential contractors, he headed straight toward me and introduced himself: "Hi, I'm God."

I half-expected a lightning bolt to hit the building. But I decided to take his lead and play along. After extending my hand, I said, "Hi, I'm Cindy. I gave birth to two of your evangelists—Luke and John."

The group laughed, and we started our meeting. I was glad that I'd found a humorous way to reply to Mr. Decider. I would have regretted *not* saying more than just my name. I would have regretted if he had stopped me with his fear tactic.

I realized that I'd rather feel immediate fear than later regret. So I acted at that meeting to avoid regret.

I've found that asking myself how I can avoid regret has often helped me decide what to do.

For instance, I had entered college with an undeclared major. I'm convinced there are two kinds of people in the world: those who know from an early age exactly what they want to do with their lives, and those who don't.

I'm in Group Number Two. I knew that I could never be happy in some majors. However, I have many interests and felt I could succeed in several areas. So when I needed to choose, I asked myself, "What would I most regret *not* studying as an undergrad?"

By imagining myself in the future and looking back, I found my answer: journalism. I knew that journalism suited me when I first walked into the classroom and I felt at home.

Asking myself how I could avoid future regret helped me act in the present for my own best interest.

***Act now
to avoid regret later—
don't let fear stop you.***

Chapter 6

When to Say 'No'

Mom never learned to drive. She relied on Dad, and when he could no longer drive safely, she'd often rely on us kids or our spouses.

One day, I'd spent the morning running errands with her, with my two-year-old in tow. It was near his naptime and I wanted to get home.

I told this to Mom. Nevertheless, when I rolled into her driveway, she asked me to do another errand for her inside the house. It was something that could have waited another time.

But I did it anyway. It was part of a familiar pattern between my mother and me.

Whenever I'd visit her, I'd tell her when I needed to go and she'd still ask me to do one more thing before I left.

So I'd reluctantly perform the errand. Then I'd feel mad at her for pushing me beyond my time constraints—*and* mad at myself for *not* saying "no" to her.

But this time was different. Back at home, while my son was napping, I thought about my feelings. I realized that my behavior was now affecting my kids. That's when I vowed to change—for their sake *and* for mine.

After reading *Codependent No More*, by Melody Beattie, I realized I couldn't change Mom's behavior. But I could change mine, and let her deal with it.

I knew Mom would still try to make me feel guilty for saying "no" to her. But I realized that I'd rather feel undeserved guilt in the moment than feel deserved resentment later on.

As expected, the next time I did errands with her, she tried to add non-urgent chores to the end of my visit. But I calmly said, "Sorry, I can't." She wasn't used to me telling her "no," so she kept asking me why I couldn't. But I just stayed calm, said good-bye, and left.

I had decided that avoiding resentment was more important to me than avoiding guilt. But more importantly, I realized that my mother's wants shouldn't outweigh my child's needs—*or* my own.

I'd like to say that, after that day, Mom stopped trying to make me feel guilty for saying "no" to her. But that's not the truth.

The truth is, whenever I'd visit, she'd *still* ask me to do things she easily could have done herself. It wasn't a matter of doing her a favor. Over the years, I had done many favors for her.

In this case, she needed to keep up her strength. She'd wanted to live on her own and avoid assisted living. So her doctor said she needed to keep doing her own daily chores. The exercise was important for her.

However, Mom wanted it both ways. She wanted to stay in her own home—yet she wanted to be treated as if she were in a facility where others would do her household chores for her.

When Mom developed pulmonary fibrosis and needed an oxygen concentrator at home, she'd rarely add distilled water to her own machine. Instead, she'd ask anyone who walked through her front door to do that chore for her—including the people who delivered her warm lunches.

Then when I'd visit, she'd ask me to fill the water and I'd say "no." "Everybody else helps me," she'd say in a hurt voice. "Why can't you? Can't you do me this *one* favor?"

"I'm not everybody else," I'd reply, reminding Mom of what her doctor had said.

Once, as I was walking out the door, she asked, "Aren't you going to stay around to see me fall while I put water in the machine?"

Of course, Mom was trying to prod me with guilt to do something I didn't need to do. I felt bad, but I said good-bye and left.

Sitting in my car, I reminded myself that Mom *could and should* do it for herself. Her doctor said so. She just didn't *want* to do it, even though it was in her own best interest to keep up her muscle strength.

But here's the irony: she acted as if it was *right for herself* not to do her own chore...but *wrong for me* not to do her chore for her. Clearly, it was a double standard.

I could *not* have helped Mom by doing her exercise for her—just the thought itself is preposterous. But if I had caved in and done it anyway, I would have felt resentful. That truly would have been a lose-lose situation.

In times past, I would *not* have included my feelings in the equation of our relationship. But now I did. I acted on the truth: My feelings counted *just as much* as my mother's feelings.

I knew I couldn't completely turn off feeling guilty. But now I understood that this story involved *more* than her guilt tactics—it *also* involved my potential resentment.

So I decided I'd rather feel Mom's undeserved guilt than my own deserved resentment.

***It's better to feel guilty
for saying "no"
than resentful
after saying "yes."***

Chapter 7

Problems with Accommodation

One night I was driving by myself on a dedicated two-lane road in a residential neighborhood. No other cars were traveling on the road and I was moving about 32 miles per hour in a 25 mph zone.

Suddenly, I saw headlights behind me. The driver seemed to be in a hurry because the car started gaining on me. As a woman alone at night, I felt uncomfortable.

Because of the tailgating, I sped up a bit more, but that didn't help. So I thought I'd avoid trouble and get out of the way by turning onto the nearest side street.

But as I turned, the other car followed me. That made me even *more* nervous. But that wasn't the end of it. Then I heard a siren and saw flashing lights.

I'd been busted for speeding by a tailgating cop. So I pulled over, stopped and rolled down my car window to talk to the officer, who checked my driver's license and registration.

Now I'm not a perfect driver, as the story shows. But I hadn't had a speeding ticket in 30 years, so he let me off with a warning. I guess I should have felt grateful. And part of me *was* grateful.

But another part of me felt bullied. A car I couldn't identify had been tailgating me at night. So I'd tried to protect myself. Not only that, I'd felt pressured to *increase* my lower level speeding to a higher level in order to avoid the tailgating.

I never thought that my gesture of accommodation—speeding up because of the tailgating car—might make my situation worse. Of course, I shouldn't have sped in the first place. But the main lesson I learned from this story was: *Don't be too accommodating.*

However, sometimes I need to learn a lesson twice. That second lesson occurred after doing a favor for Mom.

Her request seemed innocent enough: Would I please wind up her chiming clock? She said she'd just had the clock repaired, and wanted to keep using it. The clock sat on top of a cabinet. And since I was taller than Mom, it would be easier for me to wind it up than for her.

As I started winding it, she said, "Don't wind it up all the way." She said she was afraid I might break the clock by winding it too tight. Fine, I thought. After all, she'll probably ask someone else to wind it up later in the week.

So I did the favor exactly as she asked. Five days later, she called again: The clock must be broken. Would I please take her and the clock back to the repair shop?

When we got to the store, the owner examined the clock and said it was fine. The clock had stopped, he said, because it wasn't wound up enough.

Then Mom pointed to me and told the storeowner, "She's the one who didn't wind it up all the way." Ouch. Finally, I learned: *Don't be too accommodating.*

After these two incidents, I asked myself what I could do to reduce similar incidents in the future. So I decided that I would:

- Let capable people *ask directly* for what they want, and

- Avoid doing *needless* favors for difficult people.

First, capable people would need to ask me directly for what they'd want. No longer would I try to read their minds or act on their hints. After all, it's manipulative for capable people to gain my *direct* help from their *indirect* behavior.

To clarify their indirectness, I could ask: "Is there something you'd like to (ask/tell) me?" or "Why are you (asking/telling) me this?" or "What do you mean?" If they didn't clarify their indirectness, then I wouldn't take their hint—just as I shouldn't have taken the hint from the behavior of the tailgating driver.

Of course, I'm not talking about less capable people. I'm talking about people who *can* speak directly for themselves—but don't. They may not speak at all...or if they do, they may avoid asking directly for what they want. Either way, they want to receive without asking...find without seeking...walk through an open door without the effort of knocking.

For example, when Mom would visit, she'd routinely say: "Do you want to get my coat?" She tried to morph her request from what *she* wanted into what *I* wanted... instead of just asking me: "Would you please get my coat?"

It was another no-win situation. If I'd joke and say, "No, I don't," I'd look like a jerky daughter acting rude to her elderly mother. But if I got her coat without her asking directly, I'd let myself be manipulated over a silly issue.

So I hit upon the idea of rephrasing her request: "Would you like me to get your coat?" Someone who *wasn't* trying to manipulate me simply would have replied, "Yes, please." But not my mother. She replied, "If you want to."

Nevertheless, such a silly issue showed me just how far Mom would go to twist a simple action into a manipulation—and avoid owning her own request.

<u>Second, I wouldn't do any needless favors for difficult people</u>. *If* they could do something for themselves, then my answer would be "no."

They might not *want* to do it for themselves, but that's a different matter. After all, difficult people *often* want to avoid the responsibilities that match their authority. That's one of the definitions of difficult people.

Of course, in an emergency, people cannot act properly for themselves, so the situation would be different. But the clock incident was certainly no emergency. Before I took the clock back to the shop, I could have *verified for myself* if the clock actually was broken instead of taking Mom's opinion as fact. I could have tried winding it again myself.

But even when I first wound up the clock for Mom, I could have handled the situation differently. If I'd had the opportunity for a do-over, I would have told Mom: "I'll take the clock down from the cabinet, then I'll let *you* wind it up the way you like."

By acting this way, I would have helped Mom do what she *couldn't* do for herself, while still allowing her to do what she *could*—a humane and effective solution sure to please any reasonable person.

However, my Mom most likely would have replied: "Why can't you do me this *one* favor?"

Here's why: People who act difficult often turn on you after you do something for them that they could have done for themselves. After the clock incident, I decided to stop doing favors for ungrateful people.

For example, one time I saw someone who looked swamped doing a kitchen chore. So I "tried to be nice" by helping her out... but I didn't ask her first if she wanted my help. The truth is I *should* have asked her. Regardless, she wasn't grateful. She didn't see it as a favor. Instead, I later heard her criticize me to someone else: "I didn't *ask* her to do it. She *volunteered!*"

However, as the clock incident showed, *even if* difficult people ask you for help, they *still* might cause you trouble if you do them a needless favor. Why? Because instead of interpreting your action as a favor, they may view it as an insult...as an admission that you think they're incompetent.

In *Codependent No More*, Melody Beattie talks about this reaction. She explains why "rescued" people often turn against those who help them.

The reason: If you think people are *competent*, you'll let them do what they can for themselves. Instead of advising them, you'll *let them think for themselves*. Instead of acting for them, you'll *let them act on their own behalf*—even if they're slow or they don't do it the way you would.

But if you think people are *incompetent*, you'll try to save them from their own responsibilities and consequences. You may tell them how to think or you may do their work for them, as I did with the person who looked swamped.

In my experience, reasonable people view a favor as a kind gesture from one competent person to another. But difficult people see it as a confirmation of the doubts they feel about themselves. So they may blame you for the needless help you gave them—*whether or not they asked you for it.*

It's ironic: Difficult people may drop hints or ask you to do needless favors as if they are incompetent—yet they want you to treat them as if they are competent. They may be mad now *if you don't* help them—or mad later *if you do*.

In other words, you cannot win with difficult people. They set up their games so that you'll feel bad no matter what option you choose.

So when you're dealing with them, your *real* choice is: Which way do you want to feel bad? Would you rather feel guilty now for refusing them—or resentful later if you wind up doing them a needless favor?

If you choose present guilt over future resentment, here are some polite ways to tell them "no." Expect that they'll persist— and that you'll need to repeat yourself.

- "Sorry, but I can't do that."
- "Sorry, but I'd feel uncomfortable doing that."
- "I think it would be better if you did that yourself."
- "I know you can do it!"

When difficult people persist, they might play a status card, the way Mom would when she'd ask nosy questions.

For instance, it wouldn't matter if I'd ask her why she asked, or if I'd offer her a polite-but-fuzzy response. Mom would still act hurt and say: "Don't I have a right to ask? After all, I'm your mother." This was *years* after I had reached the age of majority.

Here's what I *wish* I had said: "Sure, you have a right to ask... and *I* have a right to say 'no.'" Or I could have said: "You sound as if I don't have a right to say 'no' to you."

To steel your resolve when you say "no" to difficult people, you can remind yourself about the irony of the situation: Difficult people feel *they're* entitled to ask...yet *you're* not entitled to tell them "no." They want you to consider how *they'll* feel if you refuse them...yet they didn't consider how *you'd* feel about their request in the first place.

In other words, difficult people want your relationship with them to be a one-way street—going in *their* direction. They're not concerned about being fair to you.

So don't worry if they're mad at you now. It's more important that you're not mad at yourself later.

> **Let difficult people ask you directly**
> **for what they want...**
> **and don't do them**
> **any needless favors.**

Chapter 8

Your Achilles' Heel

A couple years before Mom died, she said something to me that I'd never forget.

I'd been over at her house, helping her with chores she couldn't do for herself. She had asked me to move a small portable safe from one room to another. I remember standing in the hallway, holding that heavy box, when she started to criticize something I was doing.

I don't remember what her specific criticism was. I found that, the older Mom grew—and the more she depended on me—the more difficult she would act.

She'd *often* criticize what I did, so sometimes I'd let it run off my back and say nothing. Other times, I might try to convince her that my suggestion might help her.

If Mom wouldn't lighten up, I'd sometimes joke and say, "Yeah, I know, I'm such a bad daughter." Hearing me say that would usually jolt her out of her negativity. Realizing she'd gone too far, she'd dispute my self-deprecating remark.

So while I was standing there in the hallway holding the safe, I joked, "Yeah, I know, I'm such a heartless daughter."

But this time was different. She paused, looked at me and said, "Yes, you *are* a heartless daughter."

I was stunned. How could she seriously say that? All the car rides, errands and chores I'd done for her. All the dinner invitations I'd extended after Dad died. All the help I'd given her after she'd returned home from her hospital stays. All the arrangements I'd made for home delivery of warm meals and home visits by a doctor. Apparently, *none* of that mattered.

I finished moving the safe. Then I put on my coat, picked up my purse and told her I was leaving because I wouldn't stay when she talked to me like that.

If she had been anyone *but* my mother, I might never have talked with her again.

Back at home, I thought of all the retorts I *could* have said: "It takes one to know one" or "Now I know what you really think of me" or "I'm sorry you feel that way" or "Don't hold back. Tell me what you *really* think!"

I could have responded with a bland remark, like, "What an interesting opinion," or a more feisty reply, like, "I had no idea you were an authority on heartlessness."

But I said none of the above. Instead, I wrote in my journal. Thinking through the situation and describing it objectively helped me cut through my emotional fog. In words of black on white, I could see clearly how unfairly my mother had treated me.

Her remark still hurt. But journaling helped me see *objectively* how baseless it was. *Of course* I wasn't heartless. The fact that Mom ignored what I did for her said more about *her* than it did about me. Even when she treated me lousy, I still tried to help her with what she needed.

Journaling helped me understand my real problem: I cared about her *opinion* of me. *That* was my vulnerability—my Achilles' Heel.

After all, if my own mother could misjudge me, so could others who barely knew me. So despite herself, Mom taught me an important lesson: *Don't worry what unreasonable people think of you!*

The Talmud says, "We see things not as they are but as *we* are." Like other difficult people I've known, Mom in her older years often held opinions that had little connection with the facts. Instead, what I said or did was just an inkblot test—an excuse for her to project her own thoughts and feelings.

But when we care too much what people think of us, we allow them to control us—by allowing them to grant or withhold their approval. Difficult people take advantage of that. They *want* us to care about their opinion of us.

So if we care about others, then they may try to control us by calling us "nice" when we do what they want—or "heartless" when we don't.

If we're reasonable and intelligent, then they may try to control us by calling us "smart" when we do what they want—and when we don't, they may aggressively call us names or passively refuse to understand us.

That happened one Christmas when we gave Mom a new radio.

She was an avid radio listener, but she often told us that she found it difficult to adjust the dial and replace the batteries on her old radio.

So we gave Mom a new radio with a built-in battery that would recharge whenever she plugged it in. Then she could unplug it and move it where she wanted. The radio also sported a big round tuning dial that we thought would be easy for her to turn.

Although Mom's mind was still sharp, she acted as if she didn't understand how a radio dial worked. Her difficulty in understanding seemed particularly odd because she had grown up with radios—dials were hardly a new concept to her, even if the radio itself was new.

But Ray, my reasonable and intelligent husband, kept trying to explain to her how to use the dial. For 45 minutes, he kept going over the same information with her...and for 45 minutes, she kept saying she didn't understand how the dial worked.

Finally he gave up. So we said good-bye and left.

Later, Mom called me to say that she liked the radio—and that she figured out by herself how to use the dial.

*Don't worry
what unreasonable people
think of you.*

Chapter 9

Not-Enough Syndrome

Mom didn't always act difficult. When I was growing up, our family would weather her occasional episodes, but I also remember sharing happier times with her.

But as Mom grew older, her difficult episodes became the norm. I realize there's often a reluctant role reversal when elderly parents need the help of their more able-bodied children. But with my mother, she seemed to welcome the role reversal.

Mom had three children, all who married and had young kids of their own. She could have called on any of us for help. But I lived closest to her and worked from home as a freelance writer, so I was often the most convenient child for her to call when she wanted something.

Before Dad died, a series of small strokes had weakened him. I understand why people want to remain in their homes for as long as possible. But I believe that staying in your own home under such conditions requires essential changes within the home and within the family.

Because of Dad's condition, we kids had asked Mom to arrange for more outside help for his care. Mom and Dad had Medicare coverage and a good supplemental insurance policy.

But Mom didn't easily trust outsiders. Reluctantly, she did allow aides to help bathe Dad when he was released from the hospital after another stroke. But she didn't rearrange their furniture or add home health devices, which could have helped Dad move about more easily in his weakened state.

Mom kept everything in their house the same—but she compensated by leaning on us kids for almost all of what they needed, despite our own often-conflicting needs. As Dad grew more and more frail, Mom put me in another no-win situation.

When I was seven months' pregnant with Noah, our third child, Dad was very weak and he'd sometimes fall. So Mom would call me, asking me to pick him up off the floor. I'd feel horrible, but I'd have to say "no" because of *my* physical condition. If Ray was home, he'd drive over to help. If we couldn't help, *then* she'd ask someone else.

It was clear that Mom needed more help than we kids could provide if Dad were to stay at home. The current situation was unsustainable.

But Mom's answer to this unsustainable situation was to lecture me over the phone about how family members used to live closer to each other and help each other out.

She rejected my opinion that she needed more outside help for Dad. My opinion was invalid to her. Why? I wasn't old enough. "I've been young," she would tell me, "but you've never been old."

Ironically, though, Mom must have thought I was old enough to *help* her when she'd call. While I was pregnant, I did help my parents in other ways *besides* lifting my father off the floor. I would take them to the doctor, buy groceries and run other errands for them.

But apparently, that wasn't enough for my mother. A few days later, Mom called me again and said: "All my friends say you should be sacrificing yourself more for us."

Again I felt stunned by what she had said. But it wasn't the first time. So I had learned to write it down now and think about it later.

Surely, I thought, Mom wouldn't ask her very pregnant daughter to sacrifice herself. Oh, that's right. *She* didn't say that directly. Her friends supposedly said that, and she simply felt compelled to share that with me.

Much later, I thought of what I *could* have said to her. I could have followed her lead and talked about her friends—instead of the content of the sentence: "Now I know what your friends think."

I could have used irony: "Your friends sound so wonderfully reasonable and understanding." Or I could have stated the situation objectively: "That's quite a thing to tell someone who's seven months pregnant."

But at the time, I said nothing to her—because I was determined to say nothing I might later regret. Soon, Dad fell into a coma, and I felt even more stress.

During that time, I had a regular office visit scheduled with my obstetrician. I told her what was happening. She was concerned how stressed I was from dealing with my parents' situation. She urged me to keep drinking plenty of water.

After that, every time I filled up my water bottle, I remembered my doctor's concern for my well-being. Along with support from family and friends, that helped me cope with Dad's death and his funeral.

After Dad died, Mom developed inexplicable hearing problems while on the phone. She wasn't deaf, and never needed a hearing aid. Yet on the phone with me, she'd often vacillate between hearing every word I said and turning instantly deaf.

What was the problem? I wasn't speaking loudly enough—so she'd ask me to talk louder and louder until I was shouting. Or I wasn't speaking clearly enough—so she'd ask me to spell and respell a word she didn't understand.

By writing in my journal, I discovered Mom's pattern: she'd often turn deaf after hearing me say something she *didn't want or expect* to hear. So I tried an experiment. Sometimes I'd tell her I would hang up if she couldn't hear me…and her hearing would suddenly improve.

Even when a situation would start out fine, Mom would often act to make me look bad.

For example, when I would drive Mom to social events, like weddings or funeral receptions, I'd sit near her most of the time. But sometimes I'd walk away from the table for a few minutes by myself.

Mom would wait until I was gone, then she would ask others for help, like getting her a drink or walking her to the bathroom. Then after I'd return to the table, I'd hear Mom tell others that she needed their help because her daughter wouldn't help her.

I believe that Mom learned such behavior from her grandmother. Mom once told me how her grandmother would do little things to make her daughter-in-law look bad.

For instance, Mom said that at family gatherings, her grandmother would quietly take one of her grandsons into the kitchen and pull a button off his shirt.

Then in the dining room, while everyone was eating, her grandmother would point out the missing button on her grandson's shirt—and insinuate that her daughter-in-law had bad homemaking skills.

If difficult people *want* to make trouble for you, they will. For them, even good enough is not enough. *No* amount of trying to please them will satisfy them. So don't try!

*Accept that
you cannot satisfy
difficult people.*

Chapter 10

Staying Poised

In junior high, I played on the girls' softball team at school. Because I threw left-handed, I covered right field.

Whenever our team took the field, our coach would tell us: "Look alive out there!" That was her way of reminding us to use body language that told the batter we were ready for whatever might come our way.

It was a simple but effective lesson in biofeedback: By *looking* ready, our muscles told our brains that we *were* ready.

That lesson on body language has stayed with me to this day. It made me realize the importance of non-verbal cues—especially when dealing with difficult people.

Difficult people say or do things *designed* to provoke an emotional reaction. They want to see how you'll react—especially if you start defending yourself. If you do, then they know that they've "struck a nerve." After all, if you *didn't* feel vulnerable about what they said or did, why would you *defend* yourself?

Once you show them what triggers a reaction from you, they are likely to exploit that vulnerability again.

Their provocative words and actions are like sonic depth finders—meant to discover what's below your surface. Difficult people send out their depth finders and wait for whatever personal information you provide them, whether factual or emotional.

What can you do to *minimize* the personal information you reveal to them?

Don't defend yourself emotionally. Instead, stay calm and poised when people try to provoke you into a negative emotional reaction. For example, consider the following story.

One evening, while watching a cable news show, I saw the host interview a United States senator. The senator was under investigation for ethics violations, but evidently, he and the host had agreed that they would talk instead about a bill working its way through Congress.

However, after a perfunctory question or two about the bill, the host started asking questions about the ethics investigation. I disagree with the political leanings of that senator, but I had to admire his grace under pressure. Here's what he did:

- He <u>maintained a poker face</u>. Throughout the entire interview, his deadpan facial expression never changed.

- He <u>used a calm, low-pitched voice</u>. Not once did he sound ruffled.

- He <u>called out discrepancies</u> between the agreed topic and the actual questions.

- When he replied to the content of the out-of-bounds questions, he carefully phrased his remarks so that he <u>revealed nothing new</u> about himself.

- He played the good sport. He didn't walk off, but just <u>repeated his non-answers</u> until the interview was over.

Of course, the senator knew the interview would soon end, so he could afford to look gracious and stay until he ran out the clock. That's different from real-life situations where there's often *no* scheduled endpoint.

In real life, *we* may need to end a difficult situation ourselves, perhaps by making an excuse and leaving.

Or we may end it *before* it starts—by refusing to pick up a call, answer a knock, or open an e-mail or text message. In other words, we need to do what we can to help ourselves. We can also fortify ourselves with the following thoughts:

- Difficult behavior is *not personal*
- I can *choose* not to shrink or bloat

DIFFICULT BEHAVIOR IS NOT PERSONAL

Difficult people treat their interactions with us like a game. The *information* about us that they drop into their game is personal—but the game *itself* is not.

Their game is just as impersonal as the mail we receive from direct marketers who take their standard pitch letter and drop in our name and address, hoping we'll react to their offer.

How are difficult people different from others who know our personal information? Our friends use our personal information to *help* us—but difficult people use it for *other* goals, like: getting something from us...or undermining our self-esteem...or stopping or diverting us from what we want to do.

Their fear tactics try to stop us, while their guilt tactics try to divert us.

Difficult people are careful observers. They keep track of our interests and vulnerabilities. Based on what they know of us, they'll add elements to their game that they hope will draw us in. But if *we* don't play their game, they may look elsewhere to get what they want.

I CAN CHOOSE
NOT TO SHRINK OR BLOAT

Remember the earlier discussion about responsibility and authority? We talked about it in the context of fear and guilt tactics. The purpose of a fear tactic is to *shrink* your authority while the purpose of a guilt tactic is to *bloat* your responsibility.

So when you're with difficult people, you can refuse to shrink from fear or bloat from guilt. Even if you *feel* fearful or guilty, you can stay poised by using your imagination.

For instance, you can visualize yourself as an outline figure—a solid line that looks like your full profile as you stand tall and relaxed. You can imagine *keeping* your original solid outline figure just as it is—no more and no less.

Now imagine that fear and guilt tactics enter the picture. What's the purpose of a fear tactic? To shrink your authority. If you visualize your solid outline figure under the influence of fear, then your outline will shrink from its original size—leaving behind only a dotted line where your old shape used to be.

What's the purpose of a guilt tactic? To bloat your responsibility. If you visualize your solid outline figure under the influence of guilt, then your outline will bloat from its original size—leaving behind only a dotted line where your old shape used to be.

But you can *choose* not to shrink or bloat. Just visualize yourself keeping your *original* solid outline—even if fear or guilt tactics pressure you to change your emotional shape.

To support this mental visualization, you can use physical techniques. Here are some ideas:

- Don't touch your head or face.
- Don't fidget or use exaggerated movements or gestures.
- Keep your leg muscles relaxed and feel the blood flow in your toes.
- Breathe calmly while keeping your shoulders down—no hunching.
- Use a poker face, as the senator did so effectively.
- Keep your hands in a "no catch" position.

This is the opposite of what I'd have done in the outfield, where my body language said I was ready to catch any ball that came my way.

How do you catch something? You turn your palms out toward what you're catching, then you curl your fingers around it.

Of course, keeping your hands in "no catch" position is the exact opposite: You turn your palms in toward yourself—because you can't catch anything with the back of your hands. And you keep your fingers extended—because you can't catch anything if your fingers aren't curled.

Why is this important? These physical techniques reflect your emotional position—that you won't let yourself "catch" the negative energy difficult people project at you.

If you *can't* catch it, then you *can't* put your emotional fingerprints on their negative energy.

It's another physical technique to help you stay mentally poised—so you won't shrink or bloat emotionally or be tempted to take personally the impersonal games of difficult people.

Stay poised —
don't react to provocations.

Chapter 11

I-Messages

As a young adult, I was grateful that my parents let me move back temporarily after a job layoff. However, moving back meant I'd have to deal again with our next-door neighbors. Ever since I could remember, the husband and wife had been fussy and vocal, and I soon discovered that the years had not mellowed them.

While I was still living with my parents, I found a new job and replaced my old clunker with my first new car. It was a dark-blue sedan with a stick shift, gray vinyl seats and no air conditioning.

One weekday afternoon, while I was cleaning my car in the driveway, the man of the house came out on his front porch and yelled at me: "Can't you make any more noise, young lady?" he said sarcastically.

Over the years, our family had tried to keep the peace with these neighbors by ignoring most of their slights and digs. But this time, I took the bull by the horns. I replied: "Why are you complaining? I'm on my own property, cleaning my car in the daytime. I'm not trying to annoy you. If you think I am, that's in *your own* mind."

He grew silent and went back into the house. A week later, their family called my family to apologize.

At the time, I didn't have a name for what I had said. I just stated the situation from my point of view ("Why are you complaining?") and acknowledged his feelings ("I'm not trying to annoy you.")

I discovered later that such a response could be called an "I-Message," a name used by Donald Dinkmeyer, Sr., in his book, *Parenting Young Children*.

I think the term "I-Message" is apt. It reflects the idea that you can state your thoughts and feelings by framing them in a sentence with an "I" or a "me" that's either stated or understood.

For instance, you could say: "I didn't intend to hurt your feelings. Sorry." Compare that to this sentence: "You shouldn't feel that way. You should know that I wouldn't want to hurt your feelings."

First, you have no right telling other people how they should feel or what they should know. You have no authority to speak for what's inside the heart or mind of someone else. However, you *can* speak for what's inside your own heart and mind. That's the purpose of an I-Message.

I-Messages are *especially* useful when you need to define yourself with difficult people. For instance, you can show that you won't shrink despite the fear tactics you're facing. Here's an example: "When you raise your voice, I get distracted from what you're saying."

You can also use an I-Message to show that you won't bloat despite the guilt tactics you're facing: "I'm sorry, but I'd feel uncomfortable doing that. I think it would be best if you did that yourself."

Here are more examples of I-Messages:

- Delay a reply to unsolicited advice or group or peer pressure: *"I'll need to think about that"* or *"Let me get back with you."*

- Offer to take back gifts if receivers gripe: *"If you don't like (x), I'll take it back."*

- Go off on a tangent for nosy questions: If someone asks how much you earn, you could reply: *"I really love my job."*

- Define a tactic: *"I don't appreciate your (sarcasm/tone of voice)"* or *"I'd call that Bait and Switch"* or *"That sounds like something (Rabbit/Eeyore/Owl) would say."*

- Turn the tables on personal remarks: If someone calls you a witch, you could say: *"I didn't know you were an authority on witches."* For those who insult you and then say, "Can't you take a joke?" you could reply: *"Sure...after all, you're my friend!"*

- Call out double standards: *"Let me get this straight. It's okay for you to (x), but it's not okay for me to (x)?"*

- Interpret unkind behavior as a sign of unwellness: *"I hope you feel better"* or *"If you're (talking to me/acting) like that, you must be feeling pretty bad."*

- Don't yield if people act insulted or hurt when you say "no." They may say: *"You don't care about me"* or *"Don't be that way!"* or *"If you loved me, you would (x)"* or *"You're being selfish."* You could reply: *"I'm sorry you feel that way"* or *"I could say the same to you"* or *"If you loved me, you wouldn't (ask/tell) me that"* or *"Maybe I am."*

- Don't name-call or criticize. Just restate the facts: *"I'm on my own property, cleaning my car in the daytime. I'm not trying to annoy you."*

- Call out remarks that you find purposely rude, unkind or unreasonable: *"Excuse me?"* or *"For the record, I disagree with you"* or *"You must be joking"* or *"I'll ignore that"* or *"I won't take that personally."*

- Don't tolerate rude treatment: *"I don't like how you're (treating/talking to) me. I'm leaving."* If the person is at your house, tell him or her to leave: *"You need to leave now."*

- Use humor when people brag or act as if theirs is the only correct viewpoint: *"Oh, that's okay...I won't hold that against you."*

- Spin off a reply. For instance, if a right-handed bowler tells you, "You bowl pretty well for a left-hander," you could reply: *"Thanks. And you give pretty good compliments—for a right-hander"* or *"That sounds like a left-handed compliment."*

- Stay out of triangles: *"Leave me out of it"* or *"I'm not getting in the middle of this"* or *"I think you two can work this out yourselves."*

*I-Messages
can help you define
your thoughts and feelings.*

Chapter 12

You-Questions

Once when I was walking with a friend, we started talking about responding to people in different situations. I happened to mention a time when I told someone: "How would *you* know?"

A week later, on our next walk, my friend was excited to tell me a story of her own. She said that, as a chaperone during a school event, she had heard one boy trying to put down another boy by describing things he'd done and then saying, "He's such a (expletive)!"

So with an appropriate question mark in her voice, she replied: "And how would *you* know?" The bully was speechless.

But there was more. The other kids within earshot had just learned an important lesson about standing up to a bully. They rallied around her and said, "Good one, Mrs. (first initial)!"

My friend and I had discovered that, sometimes, the best response is a good question.

You-Questions *may* spur others to consider a different viewpoint. But that's a bonus. The *true* value of a You-Question lies in defining how *you* think.

Questions are like spices. They're most effective if used in small doses—usually no more than one or two at a time.

They can also help to clarify logical issues. The two main logical issues are Begging the Question and Ignoring the Question.

BEGGING THE QUESTION

In Begging the Question, people assert general statements without supporting them with specific points. They offer either no points or fuzzy points.

They may assume a general statement is correct without any support from specific evidence. Or they may offer an ambiguous answer that isn't specific enough.

So when you meet with assumptions and ambiguities, it's reasonable to ask about them.

For instance, for an assumption, you might ask, "Could you give me an example or two?" For an ambiguity, you could ask, "I'd like to make sure I understand. How do you define 'on time' delivery?"

You-Questions can also help when you're dealing with hearsay—people talking to you about something for which they have no direct knowledge. For example, you could say: "You're talking about my letter, but you haven't read it. Would you please read it? Then I'll be happy to talk with you about it."

IGNORING THE QUESTION

In Ignoring the Question, people offer specific points that don't answer the general question. Their points relate neither to the question nor to each other.

So it's reasonable to ask about irrelevancies and inconsistencies.

For instance, for an irrelevancy, you might say: "That's interesting, but it doesn't answer my question." For an inconsistency, you could ask, "Why are you applying the standard differently for this group compared with that group?"

In other words, questions can help you to politely confront what you think is unreasonable. For instance, you can ask: "Could you give me an example?" or "Could you explain why...?" As a reporter, I've often asked these questions.

But even for tough questions, I've found that others often cooperate more readily when I approach them in a calm and friendly way.

You-Questions can tell others that you won't shrink despite a fear tactic. So for a nosy question, you could reply, "Why do you ask?"

You-Questions can also show that you won't bloat despite a guilt tactic. So if someone hints for you to handle her problem, you could say, "That *is* a problem. What do you plan to do?"

Sometimes people use questions to hint for favors. For example, when *others* would invite Mom to a party, she'd routinely ask *me:* "Who's driving me to the party?"

But it wasn't my party, so I wouldn't know if the host already might have arranged for someone else to pick her up. It wouldn't be the first time for two people to arrive at Mom's house because she didn't tell either party that she'd also asked someone else to help her.

What's sad is that I likely would have driven her anyway. But saying "yes" *after* her tricky no-win question meant that not only would I *do* her a favor...I'd also get to *feel bad* about it—as if the only way I'd agree to help her was by trickery!

So I decided to change my response. When she'd ask me: "Who's driving me to the party?" I'd reply, "I don't know. Whom did you ask?" or "Did your host say anything about a ride?"

Here are more ways to use a You-Question:

- Ask about generalities unsupported by facts: *"Why do you say that?"* or *"What sources are you using to base your opinion?"* or *"What do you mean?"*

- Point out biased or poorly phrased questions that could put you on the spot: *"Would you care to rephrase that?"* or *"Are you (judging/criticizing) me?"*

- Turn the spotlight on someone's rude or demeaning behavior: *"Why would you (do/say) such a thing?"* or *"Are you trying to (shock me/make me mad)?"* or *"Why are you talking to me like that?"*

- Question the motive for a nosy or unusual question: *"Why do you need to know that?"* or *"Why do you ask?"*

- Call out unreasonable words or actions: *"Did you really mean to (say/do) that?"* or *"Are you trying to make me feel (guilty/scared)?"*

- Question the purpose of fault-finding: *"Do you think you're telling me something I don't know?"* or *"What is your point?"*

- Acknowledge an elephant in the room: *"Does my (gender/heritage/religion/weight/height/disease/allergy/condition/lifestyle/orientation) make you uncomfortable?"*

- Play along when people say you should know something: *"Tell me. What else should I know?"*

- Notice non-verbal cues: *"Can you tell me why you're frowning?"* or *"Why are you touching me?"* or *"Why are you talking to me in that tone?"*

- Use a question to notice your own bloopers: *"Was it something I (did/said)?"* or *"Did I just cut you off? Sorry."*

- Don't get in the middle: *"Why don't you talk to (x) yourself?"* or *"Why don't you do it yourself?"*

**Sometimes,
your best response
can be a question.**

Chapter 13

Shrug Responses

Once I wanted to schedule a party in a big banquet room. So I walked into a restaurant and the hostess greeted me at the door. I told her what I wanted. She asked me to come to the counter, where she could give me a menu and price brochure.

But getting to the customer's side of the counter was no easy task. Between me and the counter was a man in his twenties. He was sitting sprawled out, taking up more than his share of space while waiting for a pick-up order.

I looked at the hostess behind the counter. She was holding the brochure, but I saw the paper shake because her hand was trembling. I figured she knew this man and was scared of a confrontation with him.

One part of me wanted to walk out the door, but another part of me spoke up. "Excuse me," I said to him. "I need to get to the counter."

The man replied in a sarcastic voice, "You're crazy, lady!"

Coincidentally, just before driving to the restaurant, I'd been sitting in a doctor's office reading a book by Susan Forward that discussed dysfunctional relationships.

I had just finished reading the section in Forward's book that talked about using non-defensive remarks, such as: "You're entitled to your opinion."

That remark was fresh in my mind, so that's exactly what I told the man: "You're entitled to your opinion."

To my amazement, the man moved and said nothing more. I walked up to the counter and started chatting with the hostess, who (thankfully!) suggested moving our discussion away from the counter and into the banquet room.

That remark might not have worked in all situations, but it certainly worked when I needed it. What I'd said was just a bland statement of objective fact: *Of course,* he had the right to his opinion! So does *everybody!* Having the right to an opinion doesn't automatically make it true.

After returning home, I thought more deeply about why that remark was so effective. I'd acknowledged what he said—but my acknowledgment kept a neutral tone. I revealed nothing emotional *about myself.*

The best way I could describe it was the verbal equivalent of a shrug. So that's what I decided to call such responses, whether they're verbal or non-verbal. "Shrug" became my term for a *neutral acknowledgment* of what someone has said or done.

After all, acknowledging something doesn't mean you agree with it. Only *agreeing* means agreeing.

Although shrugs don't carry a negative emotional message, they *do* make a statement when we use them. Shrugs tell others that their unreasonable words or actions don't upset us.

What if I had taken personally what Mr. Sprawl said? Most likely, I would have gotten into a fight: "What do you mean, I'm crazy? *You're* the crazy one, insulting people you don't know and taking up so much space that nobody can walk around you! What kind of weirdo are you?" I shudder to think how *that* confrontation might have ended.

But of course, the reality is that Mr. Sprawl's comment said *nothing* about me—How could it? He'd never met me before! All he *really* knew about me was that I had asked him to let me pass by him so I could transact business.

In response, he said I was crazy. It was fascinating that Mr. Sprawl would react to my request with such an overblown response. *His reaction said a lot about himself.*

So, yes. He certainly was entitled to (reveal a lot about himself through) his opinion!

Regardless of how long people know us, we can choose to interpret their unreasonable behavior as a window into *themselves*—not as a mirror of *ourselves*. And when we interpret their behavior *that* way, we can look at it—and talk about it—as a neutral and objective observer.

However, I know that getting into that mindset is often easier said than done.

As a news reporter, I was trained to consider myself a neutral and objective observer. So before walking into any event, I *knew* I wouldn't take personally whatever I would witness. Even if I somehow became part of a straight news story, I would need to report neutrally and objectively what I had said or done. Just the facts, no opinion.

But *off* the job, I could easily revert to taking personally what people would say or do. Forward's advice about non-defensive responses helped me understand that I could apply my reporter mindset to my everyday life.

Without realizing it, that's what I'd done when I talked with Mr. Sprawl. Instead of reacting emotionally to his fear tactic, I just reported factually that he was entitled to his opinion. Or I could have remarked that his statement was "interesting" or "fascinating" or "unique."

And that would be *true*—because his unreasonable behavior showed that, as far as he was concerned, I was in a drama playing the role of Inkblot. So anything he revealed about himself was a projection that I could truthfully find "interesting," "fascinating" or "unique" from an objective point of view.

We can also use that "neutral and objective" mindset with ourselves. We can apologize for our own mistakes or laugh at our own pratfalls.

I went to Dominican High School in Detroit, an all girls' school that was 10 miles from my home. My mother didn't drive and couldn't pick me up. And I didn't have a car, so I'd often ride city buses to and from school.

One winter afternoon, the bus was waiting near the school for passengers to board. I wasn't first on the bus, so the floor was wet with slushy gray snow. My foot accidentally stepped into one of the puddles and I remember falling...but it felt like one of those slow-motion scenes in a movie.

I was okay. But I thought about how silly I must have looked as I fell, as well as the odd gray splotch I now sported on my slacks. So I laughed at myself and got up. In response, one of the other girls kindly remarked: "Cindy, you fall very gracefully!"

I loved that remark! After all, if we're going to fall, we might as well fall gracefully!

Laughing at myself was a non-verbal shrug. Of course, there are other non-verbal shrugs, such as ignoring, distracting, delaying a response, going off on a tangent, making an excuse and walking away, or literally shrugging and carrying on with whatever we're doing or not doing.

Verbal shrugs put that same mindset into words. Here are more examples:

- State the obvious: *"That sure is a personal remark"* or *"That sure is an out-of-the-blue question"* or *"I guess I'm not making myself clear"* or *"I hear what you're saying"* or *"That's <u>one</u> way of looking at it."*

- Disagree politely: *"I remember it differently"* or *"Is that so?"* or *"When did you get <u>that</u> idea?"* or *"I wonder why you would (tell me/say) that"* or *"I'm sorry you don't understand."*

- Agree with your adversary—hypothetically: *"Maybe I am"* or *"If you say so"* or *"Whatever"* or *"What can I say?"*

- Acknowledge even a remote possibility: *"You may be right"* or *"That's possible."*

- Show tolerance for diversity: *"To-may-to, To-mah-to"* or *"Wouldn't life be boring if we all (felt/thought) the same way?"*

- Play along with pompous people. For those who accept an apology you didn't offer: *"How generous of you!"* For those who brag: *"You're so good."*

- Play it straight with rude or brutally honest comments: *"Well, now I know what you're thinking"* or *"I guess you clarified that"* or *"I was wondering (how you'd respond/what you'd say)"* or *"Thanks for sharing."*

- Pretend to misread a slur as a compliment: *"Thank you"* or *"You're too kind"* or *"I'm glad you noticed."*

- Use humor with those who are verbally critical: *"I'm flattered by your warm words of support"* or *"Ah, you're such a charmer"* or *"Stop trying to flatter me"* or *"I resemble that remark"* or *"I guess I'm entitled to your opinion"* or *"Don't hold back. Tell me what you really think!"*

Let's return for a moment to Mr. Sprawl. Playing it straight was probably my safest bet. But I also could have joked: "I've been called worse" or "Guilty as charged" or "You discovered my secret identity."

Humor is a great way to offer others an unemotional acknowledgment of their words and actions.

***Shrugs tell others
that their words and actions
don't upset you.***

Chapter 14

Labels of 'Right' and 'Wrong'

When I was growing up, I could always predict one thing: what we *wouldn't* eat on Fridays.

Back then, meat was never on our Friday family menu. We were taught that it was a sin to eat meat on Fridays. But it wasn't just *any* sin—it was a *mortal* sin, the kind of sin that would send your soul straight to hell if you died before going to Confession.

Then suddenly, the rules changed. Never mind, we were told. Eating meat on Fridays was no longer a sin—except during Lent.

Now I think it's a healthful idea for people to vary their diet. Many people thrive on eating more fish or vegetarian meals—*any* day of the week. But I think it was inhumane and ineffective for a religion to threaten people with hell if they purposely ate meat on the "wrong" day of the week.

What was "wrong"—a *mortal* sin—was now suddenly not a big deal. But how could that be? Isn't "wrong" always "wrong"?

No. "Wrong" and "right" are merely *labels that reflect our feelings* about people and things. As feelings change, labels change. How accepted these labels become depends on who is doing the labeling.

If authorities or other opinion leaders are the labelers, then others are likely to follow. And once people start to follow, then cultural inertia makes them comfortable with the way things are.

Through the power of repetition, people start to believe that the way they think and act is "tradition" or "the truth" or the "right" way.

For every idea we hold, we can ask two questions: "Is it right or wrong?" and "Is it humane and effective?"

For instance, let's take the idea of folding clothes so they fit into a dresser.

We can approach that idea from: "Is it right or wrong?" You may decide to fold your clothes and put them in your dresser because someone in authority said that's what you should do. So you think that's "right." Or you may think it's "right" to leave your clothes in a pile on the floor because a story mentioned that your favorite rock star leaves his clothes on the floor.

Two different outcomes...but, ironically, the same "right or wrong" mindset behind them.

Now let's look at the same topic by asking the question: "Is it humane *and* effective?"

Is it effective to fold clothes so they fit in a drawer? Yes. Is it humane to fold your clothes? Yes, if there's nothing more urgent to do, like getting out of a burning house. No, if there *is* something more urgent to do. Is it effective to leave your clothes on a pile on the floor if you can easily find what you want? Yes. If you need wrinkle-free clothes? No. If you need to get out of a burning house quickly? No...it's a fire hazard and you might trip on them. Is it humane to leave your clothes on the floor if you know your roommate doesn't like it? No.

Asking "Is it humane *and* effective?" gives us an objective moral framework for decisions. It lets us look beyond labels of "right or wrong."

Why is that important? Because asking, "Is it right or wrong?" reflects our feeling—*our judgment*—about an idea. We might be conditioned to believe that something is morally "right" or "wrong" even if that conditioning makes no sense in reality.

Throughout history, people have followed a variety of subjective moral codes, depending on the culture and the era.

However, a consistent theme in these subjective codes is the "rightness" of the in-group and the "wrongness" of the out-group. What changes with different cultures and eras is who's in the in-group and who's in the out-group.

Today we, like our ancestors, also derive our ideas of "right or wrong" from our family, friends, culture, religion or groups where we belong.

So subjective moral codes can justify a double standard of behavior, depending on who is in—or not.

But an objective moral code uses only *one* standard of behavior for others and ourselves.

I believe that such an objective moral code is found in the Golden Rule. Although different cultures use different words to articulate the Golden Rule, a well-known version says: "Do unto others as you *would have* others do unto you." (Emphasis added.)

Once I had attended a parenting seminar in which all of us sat in a circle and shared our parenting ideas with the group.

One young mother told the group about her husband's parenting philosophy. Now with kids of his own, he believed it was his turn to do to his kids what his parents had done to him.

For him, parents were the in-group while kids were the out-group. That was *his* idea of "right" and "wrong."

But by practicing the Golden Rule, we can break the cycle of robotically dishing out to others what was done to us. We're not robots, in which our moral output merely equals our moral input. We're better than that.

Instead, we show our humanity when we treat others better than we were treated in the past...when we treat others humanely and effectively *despite* how they treat us.

"Being human" isn't an excuse. *It's our goal.* When we act on that belief, we leave the world a little better than how we found it.

Ignore labels
of "right" and "wrong"
and do what is
humane and effective.

Chapter 15

Balancing Head and Heart

I took formal piano lessons for nine years and learned a variety of popular and classical pieces. But during that time, the most important lesson I learned wasn't about music...it was about *myself*.

My piano teacher was Mrs. Bessie Benton Runner, a short, elderly woman with a kind twinkle in her blue eyes.

When I started lessons, both of my grandmothers had already died. So I soon adopted Mrs. Runner as a grandmotherly figure. She was patient and unflappable. She knew how to suggest songs that were challenging—but not *too* frustrating.

One year, Mrs. Runner suggested that I learn a tune called "The Dancing Dervishes" by Bernard Wagness. As usual, when introducing a song, Mrs. Runner would walk me through it so I'd have an idea how to practice the music.

She'd keep an upbeat attitude, making it seem easy for me to learn. She'd point out where the measures repeated, reminding me that I wouldn't need to relearn those sections. She'd offer ideas for fingering tricky notes. She'd also explain the Latin instructions written on the music.

For example, in "The Dancing Dervishes," Mrs. Runner pointed out where the song switched from a quick *allegretto* to a slow *lento*. At the point where the *lento* section began, she wrote on the sheet music: "Find notes—slowly."

When I first started practicing the music at home, I found it awkward to change the tempo in the middle of the song. But I decided to follow Mrs. Runner's advice, so I played the notes in the new section as if I could barely find them.

In the midst of that exercise, I suddenly thought of a metaphor. To capture the idea of that *lento* section, I imagined those dervishes dancing in a water ballet, with every twirl performed in slow motion.

That metaphor transformed the song for me into a story with notes instead of words. Suddenly, I *felt* those dervishes dancing slowly in the water! No longer was I just playing notes from my head—now those notes were *also* in my heart.

From my piano lessons, I learned that I get the best results by using *both* the technical details from my head *and* the emotional content from my heart. I can even let my feelings *guide* me—*if* I balance them with my thoughts.

We witness that graceful balance of feeling and thought when we view great works of art...hear performances of talented musicians and actors...tour functional yet beautiful buildings...see engineering marvels like cars, bridges and rockets...hear inspiring speeches...and watch the elegant form of top athletes and professional dancers.

In our everyday lives, we can also let our feelings guide us in dealing with other people *and* with ourselves.

Donald Dinkmeyer talks about this in his book, *Parenting Young Children*. He discusses the different emotions that people feel when they deal with certain misbehaviors. He encourages us to trust our feelings and use them as valuable information about the behavior of others...*and* ourselves.

Then Dinkmeyer offers ideas for responses, depending on which emotion we're feeling: hurt, anger, annoyance or frustration.

I know the intended readers for the book are parents of young children. However, I *also* found his book helpful in dealing with the behavior of adults.

For example, while reading Dinkmeyer's book, I correlated those four main emotions with my ideas on fear and guilt. Hurt and anger deal with fear, while annoyance and frustration deal with guilt.

We can feel those emotions whether others play games with us *or* whether we play games with ourselves. Regardless of why we feel those emotions, we can stop for a moment and think.

When we realize that we're feeling hurt or angry, then we know we're dealing with fear.

We can ask ourselves why we're feeling afraid...and how we can promote our own best interest despite that fear. In response, we may choose to carry on with what we're doing or to ask an effective question.

When we realize that we're feeling annoyed or frustrated, then we know we're dealing with guilt.

We can ask ourselves why we're feeling guilty...and how we can promote our own best interest despite that guilt. In response, we may choose to ignore what's annoying, distract ourselves constructively, or just stop and relax.

So thinking about our emotions can help guide our actions. By balancing our heart and head, we can deal appropriately with the difficult situations we meet.

***To respond appropriately,
balance your thoughts and feelings.***

Chapter 16

Taking Care of Yourself

On each flight, airplane passengers hear a routine list of safety reminders: Keep your seat belt buckled during take-offs and landings...stow your bags in the overhead compartment or under the seat in front of you....don't use electronic devices at designated times.

Flight attendants also remind passengers what to do if the air pressure dips and the oxygen masks drop. The capable people in the plane should put on their own masks *before* helping others aboard who are less capable.

Even if the others temporarily pass out, they will quickly revive after the capable people—*while wearing their own masks*—help the others with their masks.

But what if the capable people hold a well-intended, but misguided, sense about helping others? What if they *don't* look at the big picture?

If they start helping those less capable before putting on their own masks, then the capable people may soon pass out.

Meanwhile, the incapable people—*even with their masks on*—cannot help the others. All aboard will suffer because the capable people followed a misguided sense of duty.

That's why it's important to do what is *both* humane *and* effective. In a similar way, we need to take care of ourselves first—*especially* when we're dealing with difficult people who can suck the emotional oxygen out of a room.

Expect that difficult people won't understand why you're taking care of yourself first. After all, you can *expect* unreasonable expectations from unreasonable people.

They only look at the small picture...and they're the only ones within the frame. Their focus is on how *they're* affected when you take care of yourself.

They see a positive for you as a negative for themselves. So they may call you selfish or try to undermine what you're doing. They may even mock your efforts.

For instance, I'd been taking classes at Oakland Community College to obtain skills for another job. Mom had told a mutual friend that she wished I would devote more of my time to helping her instead of taking classes. So I knew how she felt about my return to school.

But one time on the phone, she asked me about my classes. I let down my guard, thinking that maybe Mom had developed a change of heart.

However, my bubble burst when I told her I had been studying for a big test the next day. She replied, "Isn't that cute?"

In another instance, people who start losing extra weight may also lose some of their so-called friends.

These "friends" may be jealous when others succeed or afraid that they'll look worse in comparison when they socialize with those who are slimming down.

Other "friends" may fear losing a dining companion or a fellow couch potato, so they may try to undermine the healthy progress of others by purposely offering them tempting foods or trying to sidetrack their exercise routine.

But *true* friends will support you when you take care of yourself. Your example may even inspire them to take better care of themselves. At the very least, they won't try to undermine you.

Difficult people may try paralyzing you with fear to stop you from acting in your own best interest. Act *despite* the fear.

Or they may try prodding you with guilt into doing something that's not in your best interest. Don't act *despite* the guilt.

When you're dealing with difficult people, the most important time to take care of yourself is when you least feel like it.

For instance, after dealing with a difficult person, you may feel too drained physically or emotionally to take a shower or go out for a walk.

But that's when you need *most* to break the negative inertia of an encounter with a difficult person. You need to take your focus off the difficult person and back onto yourself.

Taking care of yourself is the opposite of vanity. Here's the irony: Willful self-neglect is really a *form of vanity.* Some people may act as if they're so above their human needs that they can afford to ignore them.

Or they may act as if they're so busy and important that they don't have time to take care of themselves.

Or they may act like martyrs, seeking attention for themselves through their needlessly pitiful circumstances.

But taking care of yourself shows that you understand a simple fact: You are not God. You actually *need to put in the effort* to look and feel your best. You cannot just will that to happen.

That's why you show true humility when you *do* take the time to take care of yourself.

***Take care of
yourself first.***

Chapter 17

Forgiveness

In the midst of a Midwestern college town sat a church and its parking lot—prime real estate for out-of-town drivers looking for a place to park.

But the church knew the value of its land and posted a sign in the parking lot: "We forgive trespassers—but we also tow their cars."

I think that's an apt metaphor for the meaning of forgiveness in everyday life.

Those who would try to use us do so for their own reasons—it's not personal. Yet we cannot let trespassers keep us from using *our* space and time for *our* own purposes. So we forgive—*and* do what's reasonable to take care of ourselves.

Forgiveness means letting ourselves move on with our lives instead of being stuck emotionally at the point of their trespass or our injury.

We can stop thinking about what *they* were doing or what *they* were thinking—and start thinking about what *we* are doing and what *we* are thinking.

So forgiveness is a gift we give to ourselves. Forgiveness doesn't mean pardoning what we're not ready to pardon. But it does mean not wasting our time seeking revenge or trying to make sense of what is often senseless.

Sometimes people trespass against us for a misguided but well-intended reason. But quite often, people just know not what they do. These sins of omission or commission occur *for no objective reason* when people are under the influence of fear or guilt.

Later, if someone questions them, they may try to rationalize their behavior or blame it on us. But it's *not* about us.

When we expect people to think about or to care about what they do to us or withhold from us, then we give them the power to deny us what we are expecting, as Susan Forward discusses in her book, *Toxic Parents*.

But when we forgive others, it's like saying, "I don't expect anything from you. So you can't control me by denying what I expect."

When we forgive, we can remind ourselves that whatever people should or shouldn't have done, their trespass wasn't about us...it was about *them*. We can let God judge them—*and* allow them to face any appropriate legal or social consequences.

That includes losing our trust. That's not revenge, that's just taking care of ourselves—because forgiveness *also* means that reasonable people do what is reasonable to prevent future injuries.

When we face a conflict between what people say and how they act, we should listen to their actions instead of their words.

We cannot—and *should* not—ignore our injuries or act as if they never happened. They're part of our life story that we need to deal with emotionally. But we can help ourselves by the way we *frame* our injuries.

For instance, my siblings and I knew that our mother was often depressed. However, a few years before she died, she told us about some events from her past that we hadn't known.

That helped me to understand Mom's depression—and reframe her behavior. I realized that her difficult behavior was just an inappropriate way of advertising that she felt lousy inside. Knowing that her difficult behavior wasn't about me helped me to forgive her.

It also helped me understand that the bad doesn't erase the good. I could accept *both* her difficult behavior *and* the kind and fun things she had done for me over the years.

What she told us didn't excuse her behavior or take away her responsibility for the things she had said and done. But it *did* help me understand why her difficult episodes weren't personal.

When we forgive others, we must first acknowledge that they've injured us. After all, we don't forgive people for the *positive* things they've done.

But accepting how we've been injured helps us cope emotionally with our pain. We can put our pain in context and move on with our lives.

When we visualize our lives, we can place our injuries in the background. Just like a camera, we can change the depth of field to blur that background—and focus on our goals and how to achieve them.

We shouldn't ignore our injuries or take them out of the picture. Neither should we focus on them.

But in another sense, we can use our injuries to make the overall picture of our lives richer and more interesting—if we *blur them in the background.*

If we make our injuries too important by placing them in front of us or by focusing on them, then we let others indirectly stop us or divert us from what we want to do.

To reach our goals, we can focus our energy by doing one thing at a time. Then we can apply our energy by moving at a slow-but-steady pace. That gives us the time to think and feel *before* we act. We can assure ourselves that our actions align with our goals.

By focusing on our goals, we focus on our future—not on someone else's past behavior.

***Forgiving others
allows you
to move on with your life.***

Chapter 18

Love

For several years, I had volunteered to update the messages on the lawn marquee outside a private religious school.

This was before marquee messages were programmed electronically from inside of a building. The older marquees left message control in the hands of volunteers, who would cart a big box of plastic letters outside, remove the letters already on the board, and replace them with the letters for the new message.

One year, the school suggested that I could add an inspirational quotation on the marquee whenever the space wasn't needed for calendar reminders.

So during a week with a light schedule, I spelled out a short spiritual quotation: "We cannot earn God's love."

I had no idea what a commotion I would cause. That week, I walked into the school and someone stopped me in the hall near the school office.

She asked me where I had gotten that quotation. I told her my source, then I asked her why. She said 25 parents had called the school to complain about that message.

She said some even complained that it made them feel depressed. So I agreed to edit the message to read: "We cannot earn God's *unconditional* love."

The quotation that caused such a stir came from a meditation book called *Simply Surrender*. Author John Kirvan based the entire book on quotations from St. Therese of Lisieux.

The lawn marquee incident left a deep impression on me. I asked myself: Why would some parents have a problem with the idea that they couldn't earn God's love?

I don't have an answer. But if we *could* earn God's love, then how would we do it?

Here's my theory: If we must *earn* God's love, then we need a system, an economy, to *pay* for God's love. I imagine that our payments would consist of doing things that are "right" and not doing things that are "wrong."

Therefore, the more "right" things we do, the more "right" we would be. However, the more "wrong" things we do, the more "wrong" we would be.

I love the philosophy of St. Therese because she took personally the idea that God loved her *just as she was*—unconditionally. In his book, Kirvan focuses on Therese's conclusion that God loves us as a good parent loves a little child—a child who can do *nothing* to justify that love.

For me, that means we needn't fill up our waking hours with activities designed to prove ourselves worthy of God's love. Instead, we just need to be who we are. And who are we?

We are children of God. And God is love. Therefore, *we* are love.

We are beloved sons and daughters in whom God is well pleased. When we immerse ourselves in that understanding, our lives are changed forever. We can relax. We know we are enough—just as God made us. We don't need to be "right" or perfect. We don't need to win or get in the last word. We don't need to be appreciated or understood—though it feels nice if we are. We only need to know that God loves us and there's nothing we can do about it...*except to love others in return.*

So we shouldn't take personally the difficult behavior of others. We should only take personally when people love us—because *that* is personal...*that* is who we are.

When people act difficult, they treat us unreasonably—even when we're nice to them, they're mean to us. When people act nice, they treat us reasonably—they're nice to us when we're nice to them.

But when people love us, they don't just treat us reasonably. Yes, they're nice to us when we're nice to them. But that doesn't tell us when people love us. After all, that's just reciprocity. When people love us, they treat us reasonably even when we're not nice to them. Why do they do that? Because they see *beyond* our behavior and treat us as we *really* are—as children of the God who is Love.

As children of God, we cannot earn God's love—and we certainly cannot earn the love of others. Either people love us or they don't.

When people love us, we don't need to give them a reason for their love. *Anything* we do for them is enough. But when people don't love us, they look for reasons not to love us. *Nothing* we do for them is enough.

So we can quit trying to "make" people love us. We might earn their nice treatment, but we can never earn their love.

Love is a choice. But it's *not* a once-in-a-lifetime decision. We choose—every time we interact with others—if we'll mindfully respond with love or mindlessly react with fear or guilt.

How can we tell when people love us? We focus on their actions—*not* just their words. We notice what they do and how they treat us. By their fruits, we will know them.

When people love us, they want the best for us. They want us to take care of ourselves. They are happy for our positive changes. They may even feel inspired by them.

When people love us, they show us respect...they honor our strengths...tolerate our weaknesses...give us the benefit of the doubt...do fun things with us just to be with us....are nice to us even when we can do nothing in return....treat us with patience and kindness even when we don't "deserve" it.

Of course, we shouldn't take advantage of people when they treat us better than we "deserve." But when people love us, they don't expect us to be perfect. They understand our difficult behavior is a sign that we've forgotten who we are. They help us understand that our mistakes don't define us.

In other words, when people love us, they help us to remember who we *truly* are.

Take love
personally.

Chapter 19

The Driver's Seat

When we slip behind the wheel to drive a car, we accept responsibility for moving that car from Point A to Point B.

But even a high-performance sports car and ideal road conditions can't guarantee a safe and happy trip to Point B. What matters most is the driving style of the person behind the wheel.

In other words, it's not *what* we drive but *how* we drive that counts. As we travel the highway of life, what matters most is our style of driving.

Sooner or later, all of us will arrive at Point B. The question is whether our style of driving will leave happy memories along the way for us and for others.

How can we do that? By focusing on what's within our power. We can't always control *what* we deal with on the road, but we can control *how* we respond. We can control how we steer and how we use our brake and gas pedals.

Along the way, sometimes we need to wait, so we slow down or stop. Other times, we need to act, so we move forward or backward, switch lanes, or turn.

When we need to stop, we can wait patiently. And when we need to move, we can act kindly.

Patience and kindness. Those are the keys to love. In his book, *The Greatest Thing in the World,* Henry Drummond talks at length about patience and kindness.

In analyzing the First Book of Corinthians by St. Paul, Drummond focuses on the passage that says: "Love is patient, love is kind." Drummond describes patience as "love passive" and kindness as "love active."

So we can match active or passive love to the fear or guilt tactics we encounter on the highway of life.

Guilt is a passive tactic. People who use guilt tactics with us want to stay passive themselves while getting us to act on their own behalf. But we can match their passive guilt with our passive love—and respond with patience.

For instance, when Mom wanted me to add water to her oxygen concentrator, she used a guilt tactic with me, saying she might fall if she did that chore for herself.

However, her doctor said she needed the physical exercise involved in doing that chore. So I said "no" and let her act on her own behalf. I practiced patience with Mom in the face of her guilt tactic.

By practicing patience with others, we neutralize the jittery guilt that would prod us to act when we should let others act for themselves.

So instead of feeling annoyed or frustrated while we wait for others to act appropriately on their own behalf, we can relax and patiently do something else positive with our time. Or we can avoid the situation by steering ourselves away.

Fear is an active tactic. People who use fear tactics with us want to stay active themselves while stopping us from acting on our own behalf. But we can match their active fear with our active love—and respond with kindness.

For instance, when "Mr. Sprawl" said I was crazy for asking him to let me pass by so I could reach the restaurant counter, he used a fear tactic with me.

However, I needed to talk with the hostess. So instead of letting fear silence me, I spoke up for myself. I used a shrug response, telling him he was entitled to his opinion. I practiced kindness for myself in the face of his fear tactic.

By practicing kindness for ourselves, we neutralize the paralyzing fear that would have us stop when we should act appropriately on our own behalf.

So instead of stewing in hurt or anger because of someone else's behavior, we can act kindly for ourselves—or help someone else who *truly* needs our help.

In other words, instead of focusing on what we can't do—like changing other people—we focus on what we *can* do. For what we *cannot* control, we can be patient. For what we *can* control, we can be kind.

So waiting with patience and acting with kindness help us move toward our goals. Otherwise, fear can paralyze us from acting, and when we *do* act, guilt can misdirect our energies.

We can move toward our goals by following the advice of former President Teddy Roosevelt. We can do what we can, with what we have, where we are. That's good enough.

We're not God. We can't know our entire plan of action before we start. We just need to focus on taking *any* reasonable step toward our goal. Once we get to that spot, we can see the next reasonable step to take.

But we can't always stay in the driver's seat. We can't always be "on." We can only act effectively if we treat ourselves humanely.

That means taking good care of ourselves. We need exercise and sunshine, which are good for body *and* soul. We need to eat well and get enough sleep. We need to keep ourselves groomed and dress appropriately for the weather and the occasion. We need to balance work with rest and recreation.

We also need to do our fair share for the common goals of our family and community. That means doing some of the work *and* letting others help, too. In a group, we sometimes need to sit back and let others contribute their skills and ideas.

We can also take care of ourselves by doing our own chores. Chores aren't "beneath" us. Instead, doing chores helps us stay emotionally grounded and physically strong. When we do our own chores, we also accomplish two other things.

First, we gain a sense of accomplishment that we don't always enjoy from working with our heads. By working with our hands, we see a basket full of laundry turn into a neat pile of folded towels...we watch a sink of dirty dishes turn into a dish rack of sparkling plates...we see a dirty kitchen floor shine after we've mopped...we transform an overgrown plot of grass into a manicured carpet of green.

Second, working with our hands can give our anxious minds a break. Doing mindless physical tasks can be a welcome relief after a long stretch of work that's mentally or emotionally draining. Ironically, I often get my most useful ideas or insights while I'm washing the dishes or mopping the floor.

But sometimes, despite our best efforts to take care of ourselves, we may need someone to help us overcome depression or some other negativity we're dealing with. We can seek that help from trained and caring professionals.

We need to value ourselves whether or not we're in the driver's seat. After all, we don't live because we're worthy—we're worthy *because* we live.

When we believe that, not only can we move toward our goals—we can also enjoy the ride!

Be patient and kind...
and enjoy the ride!

Chapter 20

Happiness

Once when I was working in corporate media relations, our department bought a table's worth of tickets for a fun, after-hours dinner party—and I had the privilege of inviting two reporters to join our table for the event.

But a couple hours before the dinner, I'd developed a sore throat and fever. I felt miserable. From my house, I called my boss and explained that I was sick.

This was before cell phones were common. And I didn't have the home numbers of my guests. So I couldn't tell them that I wouldn't attend the dinner. I had to depend on my coworkers to extend my regrets and entertain my guests.

Both of the reporters had been dealt the same hand. But their reactions couldn't have been more different.

I had invited Reporter Number One because, whenever we talked on the phone, she sounded testy. So I thought that meeting her might improve our relationship. I had invited Reporter Number Two because I wanted to meet him in person after answering several of his phone calls.

After I felt better and returned to work, I called Reporter Number One to explain for myself why I wasn't at the party. But when she answered the phone, she said I had snubbed her. Then she hung up on me.

Meanwhile, before I could call Reporter Number Two, I found in my in-box his handwritten note, thanking me for the invitation and telling me how much he enjoyed the party.

Reporter Number Two enjoyed the free dinner and entertainment. But Reporter Number One was determined to be unhappy. She proved what former President Abraham Lincoln once said: "Most people are about as happy as they make up their minds to be."

We *can* make up our minds to be happy—*despite* the difficulties we encounter.

There are two paths to cheerfulness. The first is to think happy thoughts, which helps us to act cheerfully. The second is to act as if we are already cheerful, which leads us to think that we are, in fact, happy.

So our thoughts affect our actions and our actions affect our thoughts. On some days, if we want to be happy, we can "act as if" until our thoughts match our actions.

I've found that the three strategies below help me to "act as if" by focusing my thoughts on the positive:

COUNTING MY BLESSINGS

Sometimes, I need to remind myself to count my blessings, especially the gift of life...those who love me...and all the good that I enjoy.

I often find it helpful to ask myself: How would I feel if I *didn't* have (x) in my life?

I know that I tend to find what I seek. When I *look* for the positive in others and myself, I *find* more of it. In a similar way, I believe that when we're grateful, we don't just *notice* the good—we also *nurture* the good.

So if I want *more* good in my life, I need to be grateful for what's *already* good in my life.

HELPING THOSE WHO NEED MY HELP

One of the most useful ideas I learned at Wayne State University emerged from a discussion in an English class. The professor was talking about depression.

He wasn't referring to the clinical condition that responds to medication and therapy. He was talking about "the blues"—the less serious state in which we feel sad or sorry for ourselves.

He focused on the word itself, saying that it meant a "sinking in." So when we feel depressed, he said, we're "sinking in" on ourselves emotionally.

He suggested that one of the best ways to feel better is to focus our attention *outside* of ourselves. Sometimes, he said, we just feel low because we're thinking too much about our own lives. So by brightening someone else's day, we can feel happier ourselves.

We can visit with others, call them on the phone, drop them a note, do something they need help with, or give them a little something we know they might like.

We can look for little ways to do loving things, as Therese Martin of Lisieux advised.

For example, we can quietly drop a coin into a meter that's set to expire…or carry restaurant gift cards to give people on the street who ask us for food money...or simply offer others a smile when we see them.

PROMOTING HAPPY VALUES

We can also let ourselves be happy by promoting values that make us happy—values like Love, Beauty and Fun. In fact, *we can make it our mission to create more Love, Beauty and Fun in the world.*

It's easy—and understandable—to feel sad when we see problems in the world. What takes courage is to be happy *despite* the negativity we encounter.

In fact, being happy is "the greatest mortification" we can offer to God, according to Louis Evely. In his book, *Joy,* Evely says: "Truly, everything which we have closed to happiness, we have closed to God....Our sadness measures exactly our attachment to ourselves."

Happiness doesn't just "happen" to us only if all conditions are "right." After all, there'll always be *some* negativity in the world. But we cannot wait for all negativity to end before we're happy—otherwise we would never be happy.

If we stop worrying about what's "right" and focus on what's humane and effective, then we can enjoy life...here and now.

Happiness is our *choice.*

*We can choose
to be happy.*

Postscript

A Fuller Picture

I first heard this saying when I was twelve: "Maturity is the ability of children to forgive their parents." Now with children of my own, I understand more deeply the truth of that remark. As I was growing up, I sometimes found Mom's behavior annoying. Now I realize that it was often just her way of trying to show her love and to connect with me—because that's why I now do some of the same annoying things with my kids.

My relationship with Mom was not black-and-white. Looking back, I realize that Mom didn't have the resources we do today that could have helped her cope more effectively with her difficulties. Time has helped me grow more willing to give her the benefit of the doubt for those gray zones...and more willing not to take so personally the difficult behavior of someone who was feeling sick and lonely, especially in her later years.

I've included this postscript to offer you a fuller picture of my relationship with Mom. It recounts our final days together, as well as my eulogy with vignettes of happier times. Through the grace of God, the love I carried in my heart from those happier times helped me transcend the difficult moments.

To help Mom stay at home despite her physical challenges, my sister, brother and I had paid for a round-the-clock monitoring service. It tracked when Mom pressed a stationary box button after waking up and before going to bed.

The service also provided Mom with a necklace button that she could press to summon help wherever she was. Occasionally, Mom would press the necklace button and the monitoring service would call us that she had fallen. So Ray and I would go to her house and pick her up.

But one day in early January, I received a call about Mom that *wasn't* from the monitoring service. It was from the organization that delivered her warm lunches. The caller said Mom's oxygen concentrator had malfunctioned and she needed me to come over immediately.

I said I'd get there soon, but the person insisted that I hurry. She asked me if she should call an ambulance for Mom. Although I thought that sounded a bit over-the-top for a malfunctioning concentrator, I assured the caller that I would hurry over to Mom's to see what was the matter.

When I arrived, I saw that an ambulance was parked on the street, and I quickly learned that Mom was already inside. The paramedics told me that she had broken her foot, and they were now ready to take Mom to the hospital. Apparently, I had been told a white lie so I would get to Mom's quickly without making me feel frantic. I peeked in on her from the ambulance doorway. When she saw me standing there, she smiled, grateful and unusually calm.

One of the paramedics told me he thought Mom might have fallen as a complication of taking the wrong pills. Apparently, he came to this conclusion after seeing the chaotic state of Mom's kitchen table, on which she kept her medications. He urged me to help her organize her pills.

I told him that we kids had tried repeatedly to help her get organized, but she was stubborn and would always revert to her own method. Though it was messy, her method had worked for her. She didn't fall because of any confusion with her medication. She fell because she had suddenly grown weaker.

I could sense that from the night before, when I had delivered her groceries. She seemed different. When I walked in, I noticed that she hadn't taken her dirty dishes to the sink the way she normally would. After returning home, I told Ray that Mom seemed weak. She wasn't her usual feisty self. I told him, "I think she's in over her head now."

In my car, I followed the ambulance to the hospital. At a quiet moment in the emergency room, I asked Mom if she would agree now to move to an assisted living facility. To my surprise, she said "yes."

After Mom's foot was set, the hospital social worker called. She said Mom would soon be ready for outpatient rehabilitation. So on my next hospital visit, I stopped into the social worker's office to discuss which outpatient facility we would use. Then I walked into Mom's hospital room—only to find that an NPO sign had just been hung above her bed.

"Nothing by mouth," a nurse translated for me. I learned that, earlier that morning, Mom had gagged on some food. Mom couldn't eat or drink because her esophagus had enlarged and blocked her stomach. Some food had backed up into her lungs—and her lungs were already heavily strained from pulmonary fibrosis.

Unfortunately, a lunch tray was sitting by Mom's bed. The NPO had been ordered before the food staff was notified. Mom kept asking me for food from the lunch tray. I felt horrible because I couldn't give her anything on the tray. I could only repeat what the nurse had told me. Finally, the nurse took away the tray.

Later that evening, while I was fixing dinner, a doctor called me at home to say that Mom was dying. He thought I should sign the papers that night to stop additional medical interventions for Mom.

Again, I felt horribly conflicted. Part of me saw that Mom was physically weak. On the other hand, Mom was sometimes conscious when I'd see her, and then she would ask for food. But giving her food was a medical intervention. We tried a feeding tube, but it didn't work.

Soon Mom was unconscious all of the time. The medical staff repeatedly injected her with medication to slow down her racing heart. Her breathing was heavy and labored.

The next day, while I was keeping vigil at the hospital, two more doctors talked with me. They *also* told me that Mom was dying. They said she was slowly suffocating, and her body was so weak that trying to perform any additional procedures would inadvertently kill her. They could do nothing more to help her live. They urged us to place Mom in hospice.

So we did. Mom had drawn up a living will, so we honored her final wishes. That evening, surrounded by her extended family, a priest offered her last rites. She passed away peacefully with family at her side.

At Mom's funeral Mass, I offered the following eulogy. For the sake of privacy, I've blocked certain names:

"*Thank you, Fr. X and Fr. Y.*

"*Thanks to all of you here for attending our Mom's funeral. I'd also like to thank the Christian Women for reciting the rosary before Mass. The rosary was very important to Mom. I remember as a little girl seeing Mrs. Z talk to mom outside the church doors, encouraging her to join what was then the Rosary Society at St. Bartholomew's. A few years later,* when the Rosary Society merged with the Altar Society, the Christian Women's group was a big part of Mom's life. I'd especially like to thank Mr. and Mrs. N. for bringing the Eucharist to Mom every Saturday. When Mom could no longer attend Mass here, they became her main connection to St. Bart's.

"Our family has deep roots here. St. Bart's has been a big part of our family life. We attended Mass here on Sundays and often on First Fridays and First Saturdays as well. Diane, Walt and I graduated from St. Bart's Elementary School. For a while, we also attended Polish classes in the school on Saturday mornings. With Mom and Dad's encouragement, all three of us were involved in parish life, either sitting on the Parish Council or singing in the choir or serving as a cantor or lector. For a time, I also played the organ here. Ray and I were married here.

"Mom loved music. And her love of music rubbed off on her children and grandchildren. Mom was a member of the choir at St. Hyacinth's church in Detroit and for a time here at St. Bart's. She also loved to sing and to listen to other singers. I remember sometimes hearing her sing as she'd wash the dishes...a habit I picked up. She loved listening to records. One of my earliest memories was of Mom playing records before I was old enough to go to school.

"When I was four or five years old, I heard Jeanette MacDonald and Nelson Eddy as well as Guy Lombardo and his Orchestra. I also remember hearing Mom's percussion records—I loved those Latin rhythms, which is one reason I learned to play drums and percussion in high school. Record players were important to Mom. Over the years, when we would redeem trading stamps from the supermarket, we brought home record players several times. Diane and I had one of those record players in our bedroom and we used it often.

"As a little girl, I remember that Mom and Dad took us with them to vote. I recall sitting on the sidelines at the gym at Mason Elementary School, seeing Mom's legs below the curtain of the voting booth. That memory left a lasting impression on me [about the importance of voting].

"Mom loved to travel, and she visited many sites in the United States and Canada before she married Dad. She and a couple friends often joined tour groups, traveling by train to the Canadian Rockies and Quebec, and to California, Arizona, New York, Florida and Washington, D.C. When she and Dad married, they honeymooned out West at Yellowstone Park and other national sites. When we vacationed as a family, our annual trips were big events, even though we did not travel across the continent.

"Mom attended Northeastern High School in Detroit, and took courses in typing and shorthand. After graduating, she worked in a secretarial position at R.L.Polk's in downtown Detroit. After work, Mom would often take the streetcars with her friends to attend movies, concerts and plays.

"Mom carried on that tradition after starting a family. Now it was our turn to go with her to movies, concerts and plays. After events at the Fisher Theater, we would wait at the stage door to ask for autographs.

"Mom never learned to drive a car. But on days off from school, she would often take the three of us on the city bus for a trip to downtown Detroit, where we'd go to Hudson's and Crowley's. Then we'd eat at Sanders or Greenfield's Cafeteria.

"Mom arranged for Diane, Walt and me to take piano lessons. One of my fondest memories of Mom occurred in fifth grade, when I took part in the annual Grinnell Piano Festival. For several Saturdays in a row, I had Mom all to myself. During those practice weeks, Dad was working overtime and couldn't drive us, so Mom would take me on the bus to downtown Detroit. After making our usual pilgrimages to Crowley's, Hudson's and Sanders, we would walk to the Grinnell Building on Woodward so I could practice with the large group for the piano festival, which was held in Cobo Arena every summer.

"Mom was a sociable person and loved to talk on the phone. She also was not shy about asking questions. I inherited a bit of that from her, which helps when you're a reporter. Anyone who knew Mom also knew that she could be feisty...which made for some interesting conversations with her over the years.

"Mom wanted to stay in her own condo even after Dad had died, and she got her wish. Mom was comfortable with clutter. But underneath it all, she had her own way of organizing. She was very prepared for this moment, and she left complete directions for how we were to proceed with her funeral. But she could also be an enigma. At times, she acted in ways that I couldn't understand.

"However, from the calls I made notifying friends and family of Mom's passing, I gained more insight into her life as people shared their warm memories of her.

"So on behalf of Diane and Walt, I'd like to thank you for being part of her life and for sharing this chapter with us."

☥

Suggested Reading

- **Beattie, Melody.** *Codependent No More.* New York: Harper & Row/Hazelden, 1987.

- *The Catholic Study Bible.* The New American Bible with Revised New Testament. **Donald Senior,** gen. ed. New York: Oxford University Press, 1990.

- **Dinkmeyer, Don, Sr. and others.** *Parenting Young Children.* Circle Pines, Minnesota: American Guidance Service, 1997.

- **Drummond, Henry.** *The Greatest Thing in the World.* Harrington Park, New Jersey: Robert H. Sommer Publisher. No copyright given.

- **Evely, Louis.** *Joy.* New York: Herder and Herder, 1968.

- **Forward, Susan.** *Toxic Parents.* New York: Bantam Books, 1989.

- **Kirvan, John.** *Simply Surrender: Based on the Little Way of Therese of Lisieux.* Notre Dame, Indiana: Ave Maria Press, 1996.

INDEX

A

Achilles heel, 31, 32
Acting as if, 73, 76, 90
Actions louder than words, 76, 82
Air conditioning, 5-6, 47
Airplane passengers, 71
Ambiguities, 52
Ambulance, 93-94
Anger, 69, 85
Annoyance, 47, 48, 50, 69
Arizona, 97
Assisted living, 20, 94
Assumptions, 52
Authority, 9-11, 26, 32, 44, 48, 49, 64
Autographs, 98

B

Bait and Switch, 49
Beattie, Melody, ii, 20, 27
Begging the Question, 52
Behavior
    challenging versus difficult, i, 4
    non-verbal, 41, 55, 58, 60
    reasonable, i, 3, 26, 27, 33, 34, 37, 52, 53, 75, 76, 85
    rude, 25, 50, 54, 61
    undermining, 43, 72-73
    unkind, 49, 50
    unreasonable, i, 5, 6, 7, 33, 50, 53, 54, 58, 59, 60, 72
Being human, 66
Biased questions, 54
Biofeedback, 41
Bloopers, 50
Brake pedal, 83
Bullies, 13-14, 51
Bus, 60, 98

C

Cabbage roll, 3
California, 97
Camera, 77
Canadian Rockies, 97
Challenging behavior versus difficult behavior, 4
Chaperone, 51
Chores, 20-21, 27, 31, 32, 84, 86
Clock
    chiming, 24, 26, 27
    running out the, 43
Clunker, 47
Clutter, 99
Cobo Arena, 98
Codependent No More, ii, 20, 27
Community college, 72
Confession, 63
Consequences, 13, 27, 76
Corinthians, First Book of, 84
Counting blessings, 90
Crowley's, 98

D

"Dancing Dervishes, The", 67, 68
Defending yourself, 41-42
Defining yourself, 48, 50, 51, 82
Depression, 77, 79, 86, 91
Depth of field, 77
Detroit locations
    Cobo Arena, 98
    Crowley Milner & Co., 98
    Dominican High School, 60
    Fisher Theater, 98
    Greenfield's Cafeteria, 98
    Grinnell Bros. Music House, 98
    Hudson's, J. L., 98
    Mason Elementary School, Stevens T., 97
    Northeastern High School, 98
    Polk & Co., R.L., 98
    Saint Bartholomew's Parish, 96, 97
    Saint Hyacinth's Parish, 97
    Sanders, 98
    Wayne State University, 91
    Woodward Avenue, 98

Dinkmeyer, Don, Sr., ii, 48, 68, 69
Direct marketers, 43
Disagreeing politely, 61
Dominican High School, 60
Do-over, iv, 26
Drummond, Henry, ii, 84

E

Ecclesiastes, iii
Eddy, Nelson, 97
Elephant in the room, 55
Emotional window, 3, 4, 59
Energy
    focused, 78
    negative, 2-4, 46
    positive, 3
Envy. *See* Jealousy
Etch-A-Sketch, 1-2
Eulogy, 96-99
Evely, Louis, ii, 92

F

Fault-finding, 54
Favors, needless, 25, 26-29
Fear tactics, 10, 17, 44, 53, 59, 69, 73, 85
Feelings, associated with misbehavior
    anger, 69
    annoyance, 69
    frustration, 69
    hurt, 69
Fisher Theater, 98
Florida, 97
Forgiveness, 75, 76, 77
Forward, Susan, ii, 57, 59, 76
Friday meals, 63
Frustration, 69
Funeral, 37, 38, 96, 99
Future, 25, 28, 76, 78

G

Gas pedal, 83
Goals, v, 5, 10, 43, 66, 77-78, 85-86, 87
God, 17, 74, 76, 79-81, 85
Golden Rule, the, 65-66
Greatest Thing in the World, The, 84

Greenfield's Cafeteria, 98
Grinnell
    Building, 98
    Piano Festival, 98
Groups
    in, 65-66
    out, 65-66
Guilt tactics, 10, 20, 21, 22, 44-45, 48, 53, 69, 73, 84

H

Happiness, 18, 82, 83, 89-92
Hearing problem, 37-38
Hearsay, 52
Helping others, 25, 26, 27, 28, 31, 32, 35, 36, 38, 53, 54, 71-72, 91
Hints, 25, 28, 53
Hospice, 96
Hospital, 32, 36, 94-95
Hudson's, J.L., 98
Human, being, 66, 73
Humor, 50, 62
Hurt, 13, 28, 32, 48, 49, 69, 85

I

Ignoring the Question, 52-53
Inconsistencies, 53
Indirectness, 25
Inertia, 64, 73
In-group, 65-66
Inkblot, 33, 60
Irony, 6, 7, 21, 28, 36, 37, 64, 73, 86
Irrelevancies, 53

J

Jealousy, 72
Journaling, ii, iv, 32, 38
Joy, 92

K

Kindness, 27, 60, 67, 77, 82, 83, 84-85, 87
Kirvan, John, 80

L

Labels, 63-65, 66
Latin rhythms, 97
Lawn marquee, 79-80
Leaders, opinion, 64
Lessons, piano, 67-68, 98
Lincoln, Abraham, 90
Living will, 96
Lombardo, Guy, 97
Losing weight, 72-73
Love
   unconditional, 79
   versus fear or guilt, v, 81

M

MacDonald, Jeanette, 97
Marketers, direct, 43
Martin, Therese, ii, iv, 80, 91
Martyrs, 73
Mason Elementary School, Stevens T., 97
Meddlers, 10
Medical intervention, 95
Medicare, 6, 35
Mind reading, 25
Misreading a slur, 61
Mistakes, 60, 82
Mocking, 72
Monitoring service, 93
Moral codes, 65
Mortal sin, 63
Music, 67-68, 97

N

Neighbor, yelling, 47
News reporter, 53, 59, 89, 98
New York, 97
Non-defensive responses, 57, 59
Non-verbal behavior. *See* Behavior
Northeastern High School, 98
Nosiness, 28, 49, 53, 54
No-win situation, 25, 36, 53
NPO order, 95

O

Oakland Commmunity College, 72
Obstetrician, 37
One-way relationship, 29
Opinion leaders, 64
Opinions, unsupported, 54
Organizing, 9, 94, 99
Out-group, 65-66
Outside help, 35-36
Oxygen concentrator, 20, 84, 93
Oxygen masks, 71

P

Paramedics, 94
Pardoning, 75
Parenting seminar, 65
Parenting Young Children, 48, 68
Patience, 67, 82, 83-85, 87
Peer pressure, 48
Percussion, 97
Piano lessons, 67-68, 98
Pity, 5, 6, 73
Playing along, 17, 55, 61
Poker face, 42, 45
Polish classes, 96
Polk's, R.L., 98
Pompousness, 61
Pressure to reply, 48
Pulmonary fibrosis, 20, 95

Q

Quebec, 97
Questions
   Begging the, 52
   Ignoring the, 52-53

R

Radio, 33-34
Reasonable behavior. *See* Behavior
Records, 97
Regret, 17-18, 37
Relationship, one-way, 29
Repetition, 28, 43, 64

Reporter, news. *See* News reporter
Resentment, 20, 22, 28
Responsibility, 3, 9-11, 44, 77, 83
Retorts, 32
Rhythms, Latin, 97
Roosevelt, Teddy, 85
Rude behavior. *See* Behavior
Runner, Mrs. Bessie Benton, 67-68
Running out the clock, 43

S

Saint Bartholomew's Parish, 96, 97
Saint Hyacinth's Parish, 97
Saint Paul, 84
Saint Therese Martin of Lisieux, ii, iv, 80, 91
Salada Tea, ii
Sanders, 98
Saying "no", 19-20, 22, 26, 28, 36, 49
Shirkers, 10
Simply Surrender, 80
Sin, mortal, 63
Social Security, 6
Softball, 41, 45
Stage door, 98
Stamps, trading, 97
Steering, 83, 84
Stick shift, 47
Stroke, 36

T

Tactics
   fear. *See* Fear tactics
   guilt. *See* Guilt tactics
tag lines, ii
Tailgating, 23-25
Talmud, the, 33
Tolerance, 50, 61, 82
Toxic Parents, 57, 76
Trading stamps, 97
Tradition, 64, 98
Trespassers, 75

U

Unconditional love, 79
Undeclared major, 18

Undermining behavior. *See* Behavior
Unkind behavior, 49, 50
Unreasonable behavior. *See* Behavior
Unreasonable expectations, 72
Unsolicited advice, 48
Unsupported generalities, 54

V

Victim, i
Volunteer, 9, 27, 79

W

Wagness, Bernard, 67
Washington, D.C., 97
Wayne State University, 91
Will, living, 96
Woodward Avenue, 98

Y

Yelling neighbor, 47
Yellowstone National Park, 97

About the Author

Cindy Hampel has earned an award for investigative reporting from the Associated Press Society of Ohio and an award for feature writing from the Detroit Chapter of the International Association of Business Communicators.

She has reported for daily and weekly newspapers in Michigan and Ohio, served in corporate media relations, and consulted on editorial projects for nonprofit and for-profit organizations.

A graduate of Wayne State University, Cindy also has taken courses in the paralegal curriculum at Oakland Community College. She is a member of Phi Beta Kappa and Detroit Working Writers, a Detroit 300 Heritage Organization.

Cindy lives with her family in Royal Oak, Michigan.

www.ingramcontent.com/pod-product-compliance
Lightning Source LLC
Chambersburg PA
CBHW032053150426
43194CB00006B/519